The Oil & Gas Business

A Guide to Oil Investing

MICHAEL W. WRIGHT

Copyright © 2016 Wright Drilling & Exploration, Inc.

All rights reserved.

ISBN: 0-692-77526-9
ISBN-13: 978-0-692-77526-4

DISCLAIMER

Wright Drilling & Exploration Inc. offers oil and gas investment opportunities with direct oil and gas participation programs. These programs enable investors to participate in the potential cash flow and unique tax benefits associated with oil and gas investments.

There are significant risks associated with investing in oil and gas ventures. The information in this book is for general purposes only and is not a solicitation to buy or an offer to sell any securities.

Prior to investing in activity involving risks such as those involved in the oil industry, the prudent investor must do their own due diligence and research in order to make an educated decision on whether or not to make an investment.

General information in this book is not intended to be used as individual investment or tax advice. Consult your personal tax advisor concerning the current tax laws and their applicability and effect on your personal tax situation.

TABLE OF CONTENTS

Introduction   5
The Seeds of Wisdom   8
From IRS to OIL   15
About The Oil and Gas Industry   19
The American Resurgence   33
Exploration   47
Refining   80
Advantages to Investing in Oil and Gas   90
Participating Directly in Oil and Gas   96
How to Get Started   99
Contact Us   106

Introduction

The fact that you're reading this book means a couple of things for certain. You are a carbon-based life form, and you read and understand English—just like me! Beyond those obvious similarities, our backgrounds and experiences are probably somewhat different.

However, I'm guessing you are an investor, or you have an interest in becoming one. When you are done with this book, you will know everything you need to know to make an informed decision on whether or not to invest in the oil and gas industry in general, and with specific companies and individuals.

I will explain why I believe investing in oil and gas is one of the best investment opportunities available right now. I own an accounting practice doing tax work and accounting for small business owners for 26 years, and I've seen every imaginable business come across my desk.

I've seen many businesses in which people do work once and get paid over, and over, and over again through residual income. Investing in oil and gas is the best business of this kind I have ever seen. And, there are great tax benefits to the oil and gas business, discussed later in the book.

While doing accounting work for people receiving royalties, I started studying the oil and gas industry. The more I learned about it, the more I wanted to be a part of it. Along the way, I received a good education from doing other companies' books and actually invested in some oil and gas deals. I liked it so much, I decided I wanted to start my own company.

Traditionally, oil and gas investing has been reserved for a crowd closer to retirement age than not. With this book, I want to explain this business to a younger crowd, a younger market, in a way that's more fun and lighthearted—with stories mixed in explaining the benefits of oil and gas investing. One of my objectives in writing this book is an attempt to interest a younger crowd in oil and gas investing.

We are building an oil and gas company, and doing it the "right" way (okay—a bit of a play on my name). We're doing it a different way -- using different media channels to explain and demystify what oil and gas is all about, and this book is one of those channels.

Oil and gas has been given a bad reputation due to unethical companies. That's one of the stereotypes we hope to dispel.

The oil and gas industry is a speculative business, meaning when we drill, there is a chance we will not find oil. What I want people to understand is the potential reward far outweighs the risk.

If you look at this business in a logical, informed and educated manner, you'll do a lot of your own due diligence to find out whether you feel a deal is a good or a bad. When you finish this book, you will be in that position.

I want to express my gratitude to my business colleague Jim Carpenter, an oil and gas industry pro for decades, for his invaluable assistance in helping me put this book together. His insight was key to the successful completion of this project.

In the next chapter, I'll share some of my personal and business background. You'll see I had little to no exposure to the oil and gas business in my youth and formative years. And you'll also see you don't have to be born into the J.R. Ewing family to be successful in this business.

The Seeds of Wisdom

"Someone's sitting in the shade today because someone planted a tree a long time ago."
— *Warren Buffett*

When I read this statement, I reflect on the people in my past who guided me and enabled me to grow into who I am today. I think about the seeds of wisdom each person took the time to plant in me long ago and recall the actions of the role models I looked up to and made efforts to emulate. It makes me thankful for the wonderful, formative people I've been privileged to have in my life.

But I also recognize something bigger in this statement.

I believe the "shade" referred to in this quote is the legacy passed from one generation to the next. It reminds me that, as a father, I have an enormous responsibility when it comes to my own children and the legacy I pass on to them over my lifetime. Like most parents, my children and newborn grandchild changed my life. My daughter, Brooke, son Braeden, and grandson Waylon, provide the purpose and drive that pushes me to be successful and live a genuine, meaningful life.

Through my work ethic, integrity, and planning, I strive daily to ensure the legacy I pass on to my family is dynamic and sustainable.

I've built a solid foundation through my businesses and investments, and I work to make the best decisions possible for continued success. These things allow my family to live in the moment, as well as build on and prepare for the future.

Investing in oil and gas has been, unquestionably, the best decision I've made to this point to assure a thriving legacy for my family for generations. I'm a strong advocate for investing in the oil and natural gas industry because I've seen first-hand what it can deliver.

I've spent 26 years at the helm of my accounting business, M.W. Wright Co., and in all that time, I've seen and dealt with just about every type of financial situation imaginable with my clients—good and bad deals, risky ventures not worth the gamble, those you shouldn't pass up ... I've seen it all. Because of this experience, I can say without a doubt, oil and natural gas provide the best investment opportunity of any other prospect to come across my desk.

The path leading me to become involved in the industry and starting my own oil and natural gas investment company is wide. I credit many influences in my life for wisdom and guidance to this point.

Business Philosophy

I believe it takes many characteristics to be successful in business, including these ten beliefs:

1) **Anything is possible if you have the right information/knowledge.**

Information is free, in many cases, and ripe for the taking for those who want it. You must educate yourself. There's no excuse not to with the resources available today. Take the Internet, for example—

20 to 25 years ago, we didn't have it. Nowadays, you can find out anything you want to know—how to tie a tie, how to start your own business, anything, no matter how big or small—all at your fingertips. Books can be downloaded in an instant, yet this technology is constantly underutilized. Never underestimate the power of simply picking up a book and taking in the knowledge it contains. READ, read, and read—I can't stress this enough. And foster a love of reading in your children at a young age. It'll be one of the best gifts you'll ever give them.

Ultimately, it's up to you to take the first step and seek out the information you need before you can make an educated decision.

2) **Success requires vision, direction and a plan.**

A successful businessperson has a goal in mind and a plan for how he or she will achieve it—tangible action. He's also able to see the big picture and do what is necessary to control the variables he encounters. He does not *hope* he'll be successful—there is a plan and contingencies to see it through. Hope is a dangerous thing. Trying to live on hopes and dreams will only lead to disaster. Hope never comes home and hope doesn't pay the bills. So, if hope is your plan, then you have no plan.

Being an entrepreneur is an all-or-nothing endeavor. It's not only hard and time-consuming, it requires tremendous work ethic. Success relies on your full commitment. Saturday and Sunday are just regular days and 5 o'clock just another hour.

3) **Balance is a must.**

You have to put in the time and work to be successful, but you also need down time. You must find time to rest and be with your family. I've had times where I struggled with both of these to the point it caused problems in my relationships. I was a workaholic. But learning to control that is vital. I work very hard to instill the importance of this in my kids. If the time ever comes, I won't hesitate to tell them they're working too much and they need to spend time with their family.

Balance is necessary, and in the 1990s, I was not balanced. I wanted to do it all, and I had trouble not being in control of every level of my business. Back then, when I had a spare moment, I spent it looking for another business opportunity. What I probably should have done was coming home, sitting on the couch and holding my wife's hand.

You have to stop and relax every now and then and not feel guilty for taking time for yourself and your family.

4) **Trust is paramount in any relationship.**

You must be transparent with the details. If someone entrusts you with their money, you'd better protect it like it's your last dollar. Your track record, your time and your experience are where you build trust and prove yourself credible. Your reputation is one of your biggest assets.

Also, speak straight with people and deliver on your promises. If I tell you something, you can count on it. I don't say anything I don't mean. Those who know me can attest to that.

5) **The team you build can make or break you.**

Success begets success, and people emulate the traits of people they admire and with whom they spend time. I firmly believe you're only as strong as the people you surround yourself with and the team you build can make you or break you.

Success comes when everyone involved knows his or her role and is capable of performing it expertly. Any time you're the smartest person in the room, it's time to reevaluate the room. You need to surround yourself with people who are equal, if not greater, than you. You do not want a "yes man." Choosing the right people to join you on your journey is often the hardest part. But once that is done, trust is key. You chose each person because you believed he or she was the best and most competent person for a particular position, so let them prove you right. *Trust in them.* Micromanaging will almost certainly hinder a person from performing at their prime. Believe in your team, allow them to execute and trust that they'll act in the best interest of their peers.

A comprehensive team is key to making the best business decisions. When you rely on "subject matter experts" to gain the data needed, success will follow. Three key advisors you need to run a business are those representing your legal, insurance, and financial interests.

6) **Do not worry about the other guys and what they're doing**.

Competition is intrinsic to doing business. Do not lose focus of your goals by worrying about the other guys. In most trades, there is enough business to go around. I remember sitting on my granddad's couch, overhearing a conversation, and he said something that struck a chord with me: "Don't worry about what the other guy is making as long as you're making some."

Don't let greed be your downfall.

7) **Do not let past mistakes or failures steal your drive to succeed.**

There's a saying in business that the rearview mirror is clearer than the windshield. A wise businessperson will use the past, good or bad, as a guide for making comprehensive decisions going forward. Everything I have been involved in for the past 25 to 30 years has led me to the place I am now, including the opportunities I have today in the oil and gas business. It hasn't been easy, and I've had setbacks at times, but getting knocked down is part of every true success story. What you do after adversity is when your true personality shines. When you overcome the obstacles thrown your way, and still create success, people begin to view you in a different light.

I can honestly pinpoint the source of all my previous failures to not having the proper knowledge. It never came down to not trying hard enough or not putting in the work needed. No, the reason was I didn't have the right information in that situation and was unable to make the best decisions for success.

8) **Learn to prioritize.**

I believe the 80/20 rule—the adage that roughly 80 percent of the effects of something come from 20 percent of the causes—applies in all facets of business. You must adapt accordingly. Prioritizing is vital, whether it's with your money, leads, or tasks. You must know what is going to be the greatest benefit of meeting your goals.

The 80/20 rule applies to proper time management as well. Understand that time is money. As a CEO, if you spend hours doing menial tasks that could be delegated, you are selling yourself and your business short. Your priority should be focusing on the bigger picture, engaging clients and fostering growth for business.

9) **Write things down.**

I believe this is important not only in business, but in all aspects of my life. I keep journals. I write everything down in my journal and have done so for years. It's one of the best things you can provide your loved ones when you're gone, *information*.

10) **Be prepared when good fortune comes your way.**

As much as I believe your perseverance and efforts control your outcome, I also understand sometimes life is a crapshoot and it's all in the roll of the dice. But good luck or bad, the wisdom and fortitude you possess is often the difference in whether you translate your circumstances into value or have an opportunity pass you by. A serendipitous moment can be life-changing.

And I firmly believe good fortune will come everyone's way at least once in his or her life. But often it will pass a person by because that person wasn't prepared to receive it. Often, he wasn't even prepared to recognize a good opportunity right in his lap, and he certainly wasn't prepared to move on it and take action. You have to be pro-active. You must continuously build knowledge and look beyond what lies directly in front of you.

The Wright family has many successful entrepreneurs—including lawyers, ranchers and doctors, now and in the past. All their successes helped mold me for entrepreneurship.

Good fortune played a role in how I became involved in the oil and gas industry, and preparation is how I turned the opportunity into success.

In the next chapter, I'll cover particulars on how a tax accountant became an active oil and gas industry investor, and eventually the owner of an oil and gas exploration business.

From IRS to OIL

I've learned the benefits of oil and gas investments from my experiences on the accounting side and actively working in the industry.

I've been working in oil and gas accounting since the early days of my career. Through my experiences, I discovered the incredible value of a wise oil and gas investment, where the opportunity to devote a small amount of money and have a solid return from "planting that one seed" is infinite. The tax incentives and sheltered residual income cannot be matched by any other industry. I provide a detailed breakdown of the incredible tax incentives later in the book.

Armed with the knowledge I had, I immediately recognized the potential in my path. I acted on it when I was presented with the opportunity to work directly at an oil and gas company.

A chance meeting in 2014, at a golf tournament in Mississippi, opened the door and allowed me to step into the industry.

At the tournament, I was introduced to a person looking for an oil and gas accountant. He needed someone to straighten out the books at his company, which were in bad shape at the time. With my 26 years of experience, I felt confident I could help, and bring his company back to where it needed to be. We met to discuss it further once we returned to our homes. Soon, the company became a client in my accounting business.

The leadership at the company saw my work brought great value to them, more than just quality bookkeeping. So, they offered me the position of company chief financial officer.

For two years, I worked as the CFO for this oil and gas company, along with still running my accounting business. The company was having great success, I learned more and more, and I enjoyed being involved.

That led me to establish Wright Drilling & Exploration, Inc., in December 2015. Any time you get involved with a business that takes a tremendous amount of capital and you're looking for partners to come along with you (because you're not writing that check all by yourself), you better make sure you have a lot of credibility with those people.

Just like with the professionals I hired in the oil and gas business, I went out and created a board of directors who had just as much influence, if not more, in their circles than I did. With my 26 years of business experience, I surrounded the company with other people who had the same amount of experience achieving success in the oil and gas exploration business world.

We specialize in creating limited liability companies in oil drilling and exploration ventures. From the ground up, Wright Drilling is different than other oil and gas companies.

What sets us apart from others operating today, first and foremost, is we lack greed. What I mean is we maximize the opportunity for the partner by giving him or her the most percentage we possibly can for the least amount of investment. Our investors are our partners.

Our solid financial foundation also places us above the rest. Unexpected things can happen in this business, just like in any business. But if a company has a solid foundation and proper budgeting, it'll be prepared when any pressure arrives. Wright Drilling prepares for down times, so it doesn't matter if oil sells at $30 a barrel or $100 a barrel—our strong foundation safeguards our finances and keeps them secure. Our quality business principles ensure we take care of our partners who have entrusted us with their money.

Many things can affect the price of oil and gas—supply and demand, politics, the economy and numerous others. But effectively managing these risks, and being financially responsible and prepared for any downturns, are among the factors that make the difference between a company folding or holding on until things turn around.

Sometimes money can come so easy in this business many will go blind to the issues at hand and forget it can dry up as quickly as it rushed in. Many companies believe they can sell their way out of trouble in these situations, but they only dig themselves in deeper. Situations such as these are when you see a lot of "fly-by-the-seat-of-your-pants" decisions made. I've seen this many times.

Numerous oil and gas companies out there will try to gouge an investor. They'll paint a picture as pretty and lucrative as they can in order to get someone to give more money than what is actually needed to complete a job. Or, they try to negotiate a lower percentage unequal to the amount of money the investor puts into a project. To them, it's all about getting as much money as they possibly can in upfront costs.

It's hard for me to call an organization that uses those tactics an oil and gas investment company. A "money-raising company" is more appropriate. They are promoters of a project, and in this case, it just so happens to be oil and gas.

At Wright Drilling, we value and maximize the dollar. That is why transparency in my businesses is so important. I want potential investors to look at my business background and see what I have and haven't done to be successful. Looking at my past shows what I've accomplished, whatever the business, and that I've done so with integrity.

Just like with my accounting business, relationships are key in the oil and gas exploration business. When I enter a partnership, I want it to last. Legacy-building is one of my objectives, and the way I accomplish this is by earning trust and doing the job I promised. Oil and gas are not going anywhere, and it is my goal to form bonds in this business that long outlive me. My goal is to ensure investments made with Wright Drilling can endure for generations. I want our kids and grandkids to continue to build on the solid foundation of the wise investments we establish together today.

Even though the modern use of natural gas and crude oil byproducts seems relatively recent, mankind's utilization of what the industry refers to as "hydrocarbons"—organic compounds consisting entirely of hydrogen and carbon, which describes gas and oil—goes back as far as time can record. More on this in the next chapter.

About the Oil and Gas Industry

Energy Evolution

To understand the immense importance of oil in modern society, first you need to understand the path we, as humanity, have taken to get to this point. Man's relationship with fossil fuels is not new, but our ability to fully realize and harness the power and potential they possess, is a modern-day understanding.

Hydrocarbon-bearing fossil fuels have been used by civilizations for millennia. References to their uses, or even misunderstandings about them, have been found in nearly every ancient society ever studied.

Fossil fuels—namely crude oil, coal, and natural gas—have augmented mankind's progression throughout history. Though drilling and mining for fossil fuels are how we acquire the majority of fossil fuels today, pre-historic and early civilizations accessed them from naturally-occurring oil seeps and tar pits, and surface-level bituminous rocks.

The word petroleum is of Latin origins meaning "rock oil." This oily substance literally oozes from cracks in the rocks in many places, creating varying sized pools on the ground. Early man collected this crude petroleum and utilized it in many ways throughout history.

Archaeologists have discovered evidence of oil seep collecting in Native American sites in North America, where pits were dug out adjacent to the seeps and lined with wood to allow it to pool. They used the oil for medicinal purposes and other tasks in their day-to-day lives.

Findings worldwide have shown ancient civilizations also used petroleum skimmed from oil seeps in many ways, including fuel for illumination, lubrication in simple machinery, and for its adhesion qualities.

Some societies used it when constructing buildings, boats, and roads. Petroleum found in a semi-solid state is called bitumen, or as it's more commonly known, tar or asphalt. Bitumen recovered from natural deposits was used in construction, typically for roofing, and, most importantly, for building some of the world's first rudimentary paved roads. On boats, it was applied inside and outside the hull to create a waterproof barrier.

Oil seeps even served a purpose to armies in ancient battles. Warriors dipped arrows in the crude and set it ablaze before firing them in the direction of the enemy.

Flames rising from coal seams and natural gas vents have also been referenced throughout the past, many for their cultural significance. Estimates of a few natural "eternal flames" burning today have been ablaze for hundreds of years.

Though the usefulness of fossil fuels is not a new concept, only in recent times has the vast potential they contain been realized. This understanding, which brought about a new era globally toward industrialized and economic advancements, is directly attributable to fossil fuels' exothermic capacity for creating energy.

Global population has increased from 800 million in 1750 to more than 7 billion today, and fossil-fuel-based innovations have supported this exponential increase. Throughout history, as technology became more advanced and complex, a corresponding rise in energy use also occurred.

When looking at energy needs and consumption, initially, coal was a leader among fossil fuels. The Industrial Revolution spawned the need for vast amounts of energy, and coal was the primary answer—especially after the introduction of the coal-powered steam engine. Locomotives and ships powered by coal steam engines began to make it a "small world." People and large amounts of product could move faster and more efficiently than ever before. Cross-country and trans-oceanic travel became commonplace in trade. It was used to heat homes and factories and fuel boilers in electric power plants. It helped lead a boom in technological and mechanical innovations, and man's productivity became unprecedented. But coal, as it was then utilized, was not sustainable.

The turn of the 20th century neared, and the energy demands of the United States had doubled over the course of 20 years. For progress to continue, a cheaper and more convenient fossil fuel than coal became necessary.

Oil emerged as the energy source needed by the growing society. Change was now afoot.

Like coal dug from mines, obtaining oil in sufficient amounts meant drilling into subterranean deposits, then extracting the product. Advancements in drilling technology and oil well infrastructure in the mid-to-late-1800s allowed petroleum—which is abundant, easily transportable, and versatile—to become a more viable contender in meeting the world's fuel needs.

A global energy transition supporting this idea took place. Soon, oil would be king.

Oil is King

Oil. It's the driving force behind our business.

It's almost hard to fathom how a naturally-occurring dark, viscous substance taken from the ground can harness so much power and influence. From politics to technological advances, to sparking major world conflicts as well as your car's engine each day, its global impact is undeniable.

The petroleum industry is at the core of our global economy. Over the past century, it has become intertwined in almost every aspect of modern society. It is vital to the energy needs of the world and, without question, almost every person on earth would feel the effects if it ever ceased flowing.

While oil is found beneath the ground in locations all around the world, North America is where the modern petroleum industry got its start. From the earliest days in 1859 in Titusville, Pennsylvania, with Col. Edwin Drake and driller William Smith drilling North America's first successful commercial oil well (at just 69 feet total depth or "TD"), to the unparalleled spike in growth and developments in the years that followed, oil has made its mark on mankind.

Oil wells soon popped up all over the Northwest, Midwest, and along both the eastern and western seaboards. The countless numbers of operating wells contributed to supplying the United States' ever-growing demand for oil. By 1900, these domestic wells had produced more than 65 million barrels of oil.

After crude oil is pumped out of the ground, it is then refined to extract its many useful byproducts. The chief byproduct of these early oil yields was kerosene. As a much more efficient and cheaper fuel source for providing heat and light, oil-derived kerosene quickly replaced earlier versions of kerosene, which was initially made from coal and whale oil, a now-pricey commodity due to dwindling supplies. Kerosene, first distilled by Canadian geologist Abraham Gesner—a man dubbed the "Father of the Petroleum Industry"—remained the primary oil byproduct for decades. That was the case until the advent of the light bulb replaced the need for lanterns, and more homes were wired for electricity.

For half a century, the oil fields of Pennsylvania (and California following the Civil War) dominated production.

But a key discovery in 1901 in Texas, just slightly inland on the Gulf Coast catapulted oil to global prominence and allowed its vast potential to finally be realized. After previous failed drilling attempts in Beaumont atop a salt dome formation called Spindletop Hill, a gusher of gigantic, never-before-seen proportions came in.

The well was named the Lucas #1 after the persistent geologist, Anthony Lucas, who insisted the area had oil despite the naysayers. It blew uncontrolled for nine days, and inspired the "gusher" stereotype of a successful well that existed for many years. It expelled crude hundreds of feet into the air continuously in those first days, forming a small crude "lake" around the well site. Once contained, this well produced an estimated 100,000 barrels per day—more than *all* other oil wells in the U.S. *combined* at the time.

Before the discovery at Spindletop, Texas produced little oil, contributing very little compared to other oil-producing states. Most in the industry considered it an area not worth exploring.

Spindletop quickly became the highest producing oil field in the United States. In its first two years of production, the oil field yielded more than 21 million barrels of oil, a quarter of the national total.

It brought exhilaration to the industry, but also caused wild speculation and massive migration to Beaumont. Just about every type of oilman—rough necks, drillers, prospectors and businessmen (and the occasional crook or con man)—converged on the area looking for a piece of the action. More than 1,500 oil companies were registered in the year following the oil geyser. Many people became very wealthy. Land in the area sold at astronomical prices,

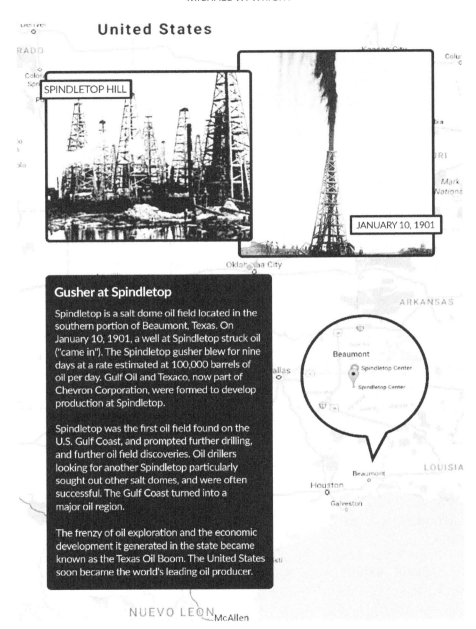

Gusher at Spindletop

Spindletop is a salt dome oil field located in the southern portion of Beaumont, Texas. On January 10, 1901, a well at Spindletop struck oil ("came in"). The Spindletop gusher blew for nine days at a rate estimated at 100,000 barrels of oil per day. Gulf Oil and Texaco, now part of Chevron Corporation, were formed to develop production at Spindletop.

Spindletop was the first oil field found on the U.S. Gulf Coast, and prompted further drilling, and further oil field discoveries. Oil drillers looking for another Spindletop particularly sought out other salt domes, and were often successful. The Gulf Coast turned into a major oil region.

The frenzy of oil exploration and the economic development it generated in the state became known as the Texas Oil Boom. The United States soon became the world's leading oil producer.

and soon a glut of wells stretched across the horizon. Because of this, production slowed, due to the large number of wells tapping into the same source.

But five years later, the area had a second boom. This time the wells were drilled much deeper to reach previously untapped pay zones, down to 5,000 feet or more TD.

A magnitude of oil-related businesses moved to the Beaumont area, or formed to support the oilfield, including transportation (trucking, pipelines and railways), storage, refineries, equipment, repairs, surveying, testing ... the list is extensive. It had cascading effects both locally and industry-wide with the creation of more companies, more innovation, and significantly more exploration.

Although a revolution in petroleum drilling and production was already in motion when the Spindletop reserves were discovered, the Texas oil field indisputably helped it gain momentum and propelled it into the modern age. The foresight and resolve of the few who envisioned a future fueled by oil made it happen.

Industry Leaders Emerge

Spindletop is credited with revolutionizing the industry and kick-starting it into a period of incredible growth. The modern innovations and technological advancements employed on its fields were key to opening the floodgates of what is the current, modern oil industry. But keep in mind the petroleum industry had been in operation for 40 years by 1900 and, by all accounts, was an established and pretty "well-oiled" enterprise in other parts of the country. Many early oil companies, mostly those operating in the fields of Pennsylvania, Ohio, and New York for example, were already experiencing astonishing growth in acquisitions and wealth.

John D. Rockefeller, one of the nation's most well-known entrepreneurs, saw the potential in oil very early on and soon established himself as an industry leader. First, he formed a refinery in Pennsylvania in 1859, and then in 1860, along with his brother and two partners, Rockefeller formed the Standard Oil Company in Ohio.

He had a vision of his company being the biggest and best. Standard Oil was an integrated business set up to run like a smooth machine. He stated his intention for his business structure was proficiency, "to unite our skill and capital." He achieved his goal by analyzing productivity and efficiency at every level for ways to improve the company's performance. With this, Standard Oil excelled in areas of research, transportation, sales, and acquisitions.

As most keen oilmen and companies did, Rockefeller employed geologists and technical experts on his crews during research and exploration phases of pre-drilling and during the well-drilling process. But he also went a step further and depended on scientific experts following the drilling and collection processes. His company was (most likely) the first to hire teams of chemists and scientists to research the oil products and develop ways to improve it throughout the refinement process.

Realizing the value of pipelines to transport oil, he invested in as many pipelines as possible. Within 10 years, Rockefeller owned the majority of all existing oil pipelines in the United States. By 1870, Standard Oil was the dominant oil firm in the country's northeast region, and ranked as one of the world's greatest corporations.

He also expanded his company by purchasing many small oil firms on the West Coast and, at the turn of the century, he combined them to form Pacific Oil. Today, Pacific Oil is known by a more familiar name – Chevron.

Rockefeller had incredible business instincts and skills unmatched when it came to organizing companies. But many of his tactics were seen as cutthroat and caused controversy. He dealt with competition by either underselling them to the point they couldn't compete or he bought them outright and absorb the business. In just a few years, his expanding oil companies and majority control of 85 to 90 percent of the pipelines made competition difficult for smaller producers. As a result, many were forced to sell their businesses, which Rockefeller and Standard Oil happily took off their hands.

The expansion of Standard Oil was both vertical and horizontal, into all levels of the oil industry from production, transport, refining and distribution. In 1882, Rockefeller combined all the companies in his vast oil empire and created the Standard Oil Trust as one large, encompassing organization. It had become too big, by most opinions. Standard Oil, in effect, controlled the oil industry for nearly 30 years. Its business practices were viewed by most as largely unfair because no one could compete with the oil giant. The Supreme Court agreed. In 1911, it declared Standard Oil (by then called Standard Oil Company of New Jersey) a monopoly in violation of the Sherman Antitrust Act. Part of the Supreme Court ruling stated the company had to split into 34 smaller, independently-owned companies.

This Supreme Court ruling and the discovery at Spindletop helped usher in a new era for competition in the American oil industry, and many new major players emerged.

A large number of major oil corporations were formed as a result of Spindletop, many of whom remain global leaders today. These companies provided the competition needed to ensure Standard Oil could no longer control the market. Gulf Oil Corporation, the Magnolia Petroleum Company (later known as Mobil, before merging with Exxon in 1999 to become ExxonMobil), the Texas Company (renamed Texaco), and the American Gasoline Company (became Shell in 1914) are a few examples of the corporations to emerge at that time.

Demand Increases

Automobiles brought about massive changes for the petroleum industry.

Modern automobiles were invented in the late 1800s. They were initially cost-prohibitive for most families. Until Henry Ford's mass-produced, affordable Model T was introduced in 1908 then cars became widely available and popular in the United States. The automobile was an important milestone, but not only for oil. It also drove economic growth and prosperity across the United States. A car provided its owners with independence, maneuverability, and, arguably most important, opportunity.

An explosion in the oil industry was sparked by consumer demand for gasoline thanks to widespread car ownership. Cars ran via a gasoline-powered internal combustion engine, thereby greatly increasing the United States' need for gasoline as a fuel. By 1911, the main byproduct of oil shifted from kerosene to gasoline.

A new, mechanized military also emerged around this time as a result of advancements brought about by oil. Proficient mobile warfare became fundamental, and the internal combustion engine helped lead the charge. Airplanes, trucks, tanks and submarines were all updated as part of United States' expanded military inventory and all powered by oil. Vehicles and ships moved faster and travelled farther with fewer resupply stops. Battlegrounds of the future would no longer be fought man vs. man. They would be engaged by man and his machines. This meant a stable, abundant supply of oil was now vital to national security.

World War I was when this first became evident, with strategic oil resources and the ability to move large troop numbers having a critical impact in its outcome.

At the time, United States companies produced (and/or in control of) nearly 70 percent of the world's oil supply. About the same time, automobiles became popular in the United States, and massive oil reserves were discovered in the Middle East. Several American-owned oil companies, using their knowledge of oil exploration and extraction methods, secured the rights to numerous oil leases in this region. It was not until WWI that many of our rival nations began to truly see the value in access to these strategic reserves.

Great Britain, almost wholly dependent on oil imports, faced severe oil shortages during the war and turned to the United States, its ally, for assistance. Germany did not have this advantage, and it proved a hindrance at decisive points in combat.

Access to oil proved greatly advantageous on the battlefield during this war and in all wars and conflicts that have followed.

World War II reinforced the oil industry as a key American resource. During which, our oil domestic reserves were almost depleted as the U.S. supplied nearly six billion barrels of oil to support the effort. Due to the intense need for oil to fuel military equipment, the war prompted the government to enact gasoline rationing and pricing control throughout the country. The American populace began to understand our petroleum supplies were not unlimited.

This domestic energy crisis highlighted the country's need to obtain a steady and dependable supply of oil. Following WWII, securing oil became a priority and resulted in many petroleum policies being put into place, both foreign and domestic.

Not long after the U.S. and the U.K. signed the Anglo-American Petroleum Agreement, which split the oil in Persia, Iraq, Kuwait, and Saudi Arabia, these oil-producing nations realized the value of the resources within their borders. They later forced renegotiations of their oil contracts and used oil to exert political influence.

But many major energy crises soon followed. First, in 1950 with the Iranian crisis, then in 1956 the Suez crisis. But nowhere was this felt greater than with the western oil embargo in 1973. This embargo caused oil prices around the world to skyrocket and impacted the economy. It also forced western nations, the U.S. in particular, to seek out and secure other petroleum resources.

Oil is the most important consideration in America's Middle Eastern and other foreign policies.

OPEC

The Organization of Oil Exporting Countries, or OPEC, was formed in Baghdad in 1960 by countries seeking to protect their interests in the oil market. Until that point, the oil market had been mostly dominated by the industry's "Seven Sisters"—oil majors maintained largely by United States companies. The founding members of this intergovernmental organization were Iran, Iraq, Kuwait, Saudi Arabia and Venezuela. The mission of OPEC was to coordinate and unify petroleum policies among member nations, to secure producers with fair and stable prices, to maintain economic and steady supplies to buyers, and ensure fair returns to investors.

Many additional countries joined OPEC over the past decades since its formation, including Qatar, the United Arab Emirates, Libya and others.

OPEC asserted rights to sovereignty over natural resources contained within its nations' borders in the name of national development. By 1970, member nations had taken control of their respective oil industries, and those within this alliance influenced global oil pricing.

Huge global oil price spikes followed, most significantly following the oil embargo against western nations in 1973—which caused prices to quadruple—and the Iranian Revolution in 1979.

Prices continued to fluctuate according to supply and demand. But in 1986, prices crashed. This led to OPEC establishing a group production ceiling among its members, along with opening dialogue between OPEC and non-OPEC nations for stability and fairness in pricing.

The 1990s were plagued by volatility in the region, leading to weak prices for oil. Even so, by the 1990s and early 2000s, OPEC nations had become the prominent supporter of the global oil sector. But escalating social unrest affected supply and demand during this time.

In late 2014, speculation and overproduction within the member nations contributed to a price crash worldwide, and by mid-2016, the price of a barrel of oil had dropped more than 70 percent from a high of $112 in June of 2014.

OPEC has been the strong-arm in the global oil industry for a while. It still has a lot of influence, but the advent the technological advances such as fracking are a boon in every way you can look at them. They make oil and gas more affordable, and that's good for the global economy.

If fracking and other similar innovations hadn't come along, the "pin-cushion" oil and gas fields we already have (they look like pin cushions because there's so many vertical wells drilled in them already) would continue. Companies would drill more and more in-field wells diminishing expected ultimate recoveries. But they would be economically feasible because of the effects of supply and demand. The supply has gone down, while the demand stays the same.

OPEC doesn't carry the big stick it once did. Its fields are all just traditional oil fields, very easy to produce. It's just amazing the kind of production they get out of those fields. We have our big oil field zones in the United States, like the East Texas field, the Yates field in West Texas, and Prudhoe Bay in Alaska. But the Middle Eastern countries have production that makes our United States mainstays look like little tiny fields with modest rates.

The Middle Eastern fields have produced for many years, and they're starting to deplete. They still have capacity, but there's water encroachment. (As oil is pumped out of an underground reservoir, something takes its place. In this case, it's water.)

Ultimately, those fields will still produce profits for a very, very long time because of the quality of the reservoirs and the extraction rates they get out of those reservoirs. But they are depleting, because hydrocarbons do not regenerate. They will get more water production and smaller oil ratio of what is pumped out of the ground over time. As that trend continues, the OPEC nations will start looking at the unconventional methods that have invigorated the industry here in the U.S.

Will they be blessed the same way the United States has been, with shales that have turned out to be a real windfall? Shales are expensive to drill and complete, but the profits on them aren't so good and they destroy the conventional markets. There's still plenty of conventional oil and gas drilling to do for many decades, even with the advent of all the new technology and methods, some of which you'll learn about next.

The American Resurgence

"It's not a surprise that our fracking technology has helped turn American gas markets upside down. We were confident in its upside potential. What's surprising is how quickly it's happening."

— *George Mitchell*

In the past two decades, there has been a major resurgence in the profitability and productivity of the oil and gas industry in the United States, and it has occurred primarily due to major innovations in geologic technology.

One of the primary innovations has been in a practice you almost certainly have heard of, hydraulic fracturing, or "fracking"—a well-stimulation technique in which rock is fractured by pressurized liquid. The process involves the high-pressure injection of "fracking fluid" (primarily salt water, containing sand, treated sand or man-made ceramic materials, designed to keep an induced hydraulic fracture open, also known as "proppants") into a wellbore. The high-pressure injection creates cracks in the deep-rock formations through which natural gas, petroleum, and brine will flow more freely. When the hydraulic pressure is removed from the well, the proppants hold the fractures open, allowing gas and oil deposits to flow more freely to the drilled wellbore. This process allows

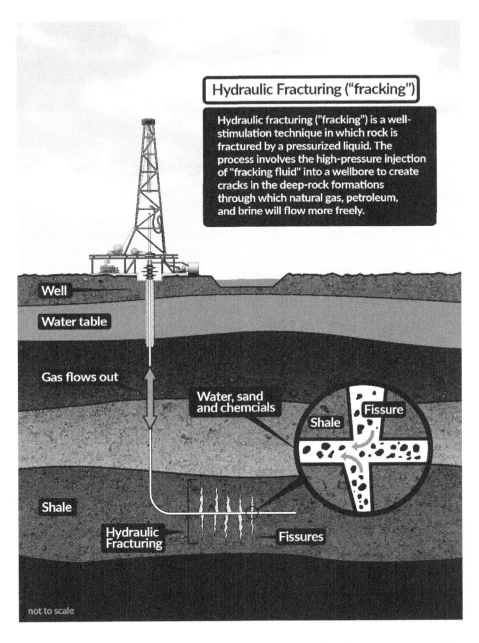

recovery of more product from existing wells than was possible prior to its implementation.

Hydraulic fracturing began as an experiment in 1947, and the first commercially successful application followed in 1950. According to the U.S. Department of Energy, at least two million oil and gas wells in the U.S. had been hydraulically fractured as of 2013. Of new wells being drilled, up to 95 percent are hydraulically fractured. The output from these wells makes up 43 percent of the oil production and 67 percent of the natural gas production in the United States.

When driving in mountainous areas, you'll sometimes see rock faces along the side of the road with water coming out of fractures, even when the surroundings are quite dry. Rock fractures have more permeability and more flow than unfractured rock, and sights like that gave people in our industry ideas. In the earliest days, putting dynamite down wellbores was the first method of fracking attempted, and that worked in some cases. The explosion fractured the rock at the bottom of the well, and it actually improved production.

Oil and gas exploration engineering has come of age over the last 50 years, and in particular, the last 30. Within the last 30 years, no one—not even the engineers—knew the true extent of the awesome leaps and bounds they had made technologically. Nor did they know these advances would lead to the boom we've recently seen.

The magic year was 1997. George Mitchell, one of the leading oil producers in Texas, had been looking for a successful project in an unlikely place—the Barnett Shale, a thick layer of rock, thousands of square miles in area, located deep under the land around Fort Worth, Texas. For years, companies had been harvesting oil and gas from both above and below a layer of highly-dense shale rock. Mitchell decided to drill into the shale layer and frack it.

For 15 years, the results were indifferent. But in 1997, one of the fracked shale wells produced enough natural gas to become

profitable over the long term. It took 15 years of fracking attempt after fracking attempt by Mitchell's company before the 1997 attempt finally put him over the hump to where he actually made a little bit of profit on those wells. Since then, the innovation in fracking has led to more than 30 percent of the U.S. production of natural gas coming from shale, which had previously been unproductive and unprofitable.

Mitchell had all this capital tied up in pipeline and other infrastructure in the Fort Worth basin, and he sat there watching the production wind down. He was an engineer but, first and foremost, he was a capitalist faced with a predicament. He could either watch all this infrastructure he had built turn into a rust bucket, or he could figure out something else around that area to produce. He did the latter, to the benefit of the entire industry.

Prior to 1997, trying to get production out of a shale deposit was a desperate and hopeless attempt for production. That all changed with the breakthrough by Mitchell's company, and previously largely impermeable geologic formations of shale, sandstone and others became possible profit centers.

You may have also heard about the sudden surge in oil and gas production in North Dakota in recent years. It's in an area called the Bakken Formation, which stretches into Montana, North Dakota, and Saskatchewan and Manitoba in Canada. The area was drilled for years, but it's been the many technological advances of recent decades that have made the extraction of what is estimated in the billions of barrels of oil from that area more profitable.

What they found in the Bakken is a shale formation at the top of an anticline, a type of subsurface geologic fold in an arch-like shape with the oldest beds at its core. Think of it this way: Imagine using both your hands to hold a sliced loaf of bread. If flexed upward, you see spaces open on the top of the bread where the slices were made. On the very bottom, it's actually compressed. Somewhere in there, there's a neutral surface where neither compression nor extension happens.

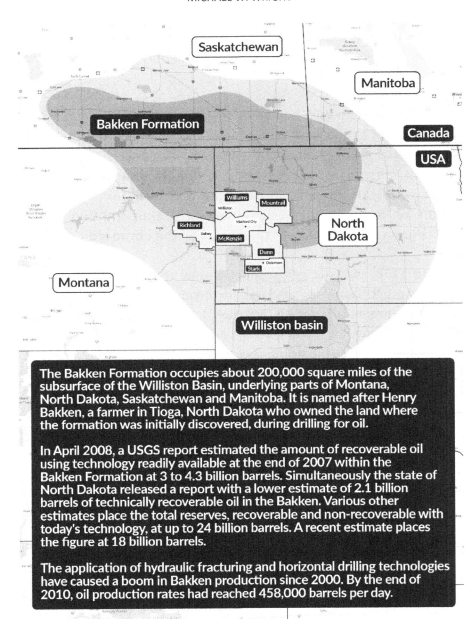

The Bakken Formation occupies about 200,000 square miles of the subsurface of the Williston Basin, underlying parts of Montana, North Dakota, Saskatchewan and Manitoba. It is named after Henry Bakken, a farmer in Tioga, North Dakota who owned the land where the formation was initially discovered, during drilling for oil.

In April 2008, a USGS report estimated the amount of recoverable oil using technology readily available at the end of 2007 within the Bakken Formation at 3 to 4.3 billion barrels. Simultaneously the state of North Dakota released a report with a lower estimate of 2.1 billion barrels of technically recoverable oil in the Bakken. Various other estimates place the total reserves, recoverable and non-recoverable with today's technology, at up to 24 billion barrels. A recent estimate places the figure at 18 billion barrels.

The application of hydraulic fracturing and horizontal drilling technologies have caused a boom in Bakken production since 2000. By the end of 2010, oil production rates had reached 458,000 barrels per day.

On the Bakken Formation, originally extension happened and it created these fractures. Plenty of oil existed in the Bakken Formation, which charged up those open fractures. They drilled into it and boom, they found fractures. What's in the fractures usually depletes fairly quickly—it comes out pretty quick, and it's done.

That early production from those open fractures on the top of that anticline, in the way of an analogy, was apples. What they're doing now, trying to frack it, is oranges. They are two different things. (See the illustration on the next page for more explanation of an anticline.)

Horizontal Drilling

Post-1997, people started taking notice of what was going on in the Barnett Formation. They realized they could drill through it horizontally and pull out hydrocarbons, even though it was a tight reservoir.

("Tight" is the term commonly used to refer to low permeability reservoirs that produce mainly dry natural gas. Many of the low permeability reservoirs developed in the past are sandstone, but significant quantities of gas are also produced from low permeability carbonates, shales, and coal seams.)

Most people don't even consider it possible to drill any way other than vertically, and particularly at great depths. What's the advantage of horizontal drilling? Let's say you have a reservoir 50 feet thick, and you drill a vertical well down through it. You have 50 feet of wellbore exposure in that reservoir. It gives you whatever it can give. If it's a really tight reservoir, like shale, it only gives you 50 feet of penetration to extract oil from. You might have to frack it, so you may get 500 additional feet with your frack. You'll produce what you were able to frack into radially, 500 feet out.

You produce it, and it's done producing. All the money you spent in drilling that vertical well, it's sunk and you get whatever you get out. That's your economics equation: How much did it cost to drill and

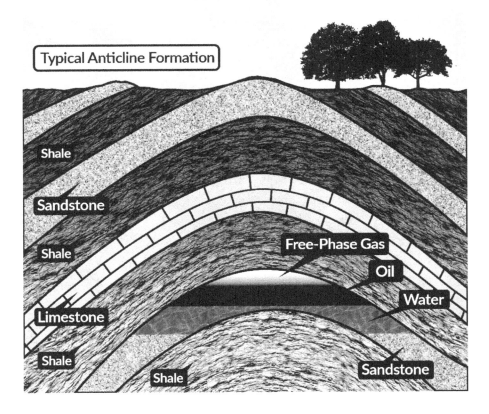

complete this thing? Am I going to make more in the way of product than I spent in the attempt to get the product?

When things went horizontal in the Bakken Formation, they drilled vertically down approximately 10,000 feet. The cost is close to the same whether you drill vertically or whether go horizontal.

But there's another magical thing that happened with horizontal drilling: When you drill vertically, you might drill 500 feet a day, maybe even 1,000 feet a day in some really unconsolidated rock—young stuff. But most of the time, vertical drilling into older more settled rock is about 100 feet a day of penetration. Do the math. However deep your well, at 100 feet a day, it'll take you that length of time just to get down to the reservoir. To get 10,000 feet deep at 100 feet per day will take 100 days. (See illustration, next page.)

When you go horizontal, it's different. Here's why. Shales are kind of like playing cards piling up in little platelets. When you're drilling down through that shale vertically, it's almost like drilling through a deck of playing cards on a table with a small drill bit. The cards will spin. They're not going to break and chip off. It's more difficult to drill through the entire deck without problems.

When you go horizontal, continue to imagine the deck of cards—except now, instead of drilling from the top, imagine drilling through the side with a small drill bit. Much easier and less resistance, right? Let's assume it has a lot of weight over it, so it will maintain its integrity.

When you drill through it, now, you cut through it a whole lot better, a whole lot more efficiently with the drill bit because it's not spinning. You're getting a good cut, and you're able to chip off those cards a whole lot better when you drill from the side of the deck than drilling on top of the deck.

With this reduced friction, instead of drilling 100 feet a day vertically, you might drill 1,000 feet a day horizontally. Say this underground reservoir at 10,000 feet below the surface is 100 feet

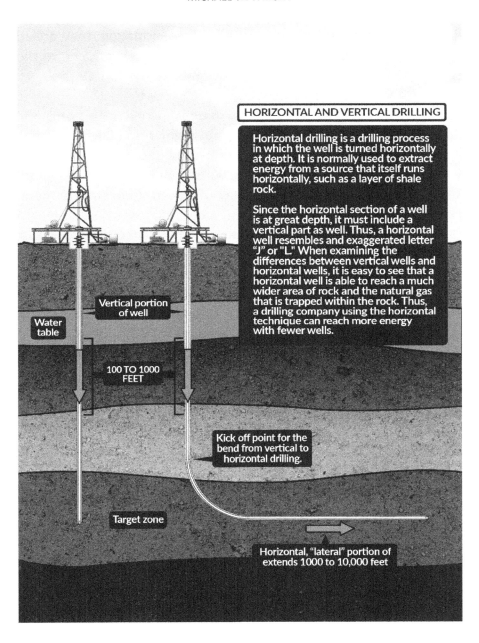

thick. It would take you 100 days to drill to the reservoir, and another day to drill into the reservoir.

When you go horizontal, and you drill through it at 1,000 feet a day (instead of 100 feet per day vertically), now you have only one day's time invested, one day's rig cost, one day's fuel, but you've got 10 times more reservoir exposed to the wellbore. The next day, you can drill another 1,000 feet, and then you have 20 times more exposure. The next day, you can drill another 1,000. You can go out 10,000 feet, so his 100-foot thick reservoir, since you drilled through it horizontally, becomes a 10,000-feet-thick opportunity.

Now you have 10,000 feet of reservoir to feed oil or gas to you instead of just 100 feet of reservoir. It's like night and day. It costs a whole lot of money to drill one of those wells, but it has a better chance of making a profit. By drilling horizontally, you turned the well on its ear. Now, all that rock with oil in it is exposed to your wellbore. But if it was just a vertical well, you might not get much recovery. You get whatever's close around your wellbore in that vertical well. When you go horizontal, you can get approximately 10,000 feet worth. When you frack it, you get 500 feet on all sides of the frack, going out into the shale. The last 10 years had been really phenomenal.

Shale Now Yields More Hydrocarbons

As mentioned earlier, the oil industry's been around since 1858, and it really started getting big after the Spindletop well discovery in Texas in 1901. During all that time, for the most part, up until 1997, the potential of certain tight sand reservoirs, shale reservoirs—in the minds of industry leaders and experts would have been, "You can't produce in that type of sand, and you can't produce out of that shale. Ain't going to happen." I'm not talking 80 percent of the experts. I'm talking unanimous. Everyone. Every petroleum engineer, every geologist, every geophysicist, every petrophysicist. Every one of them would have agreed.

As recently as 13 years ago, even after the Barnett Shale was successful in producing gas, the consensus of opinion amongst geoscientists and engineers was still you could never do the same thing with oil. The reason is because of the permeability of the shale to oil, you can't get enough flow. They were wrong on that, too. It's been a real education in recent years, and all because of the advances in horsepower and fracking.

What the Frack?

There's a group of people out there who don't understand fracking other than the fact that, for whatever reason, their politics or whatever, they hate it. To them, fracking is bad. You'll see them wearing t-shirts out in Hollywood that say, "No fracking," or "What the frack?"

The last thing any operator wants to do is have a frack go off other than where they intended, down in the tight reservoir. Why? Because it would be a big waste of money to him or her. In the world of capitalism, the worst sin you can ever commit is to waste money. All of us capitalists have a built-in incentive to never, ever frack the wrong thing.

We don't ever want to get it in the water table. The only way possible it could contaminate the water table, which is where most drinking and potable water comes from, is if the wellbore's surface casing fails and the next drilling liner fails when you put the frack on it. In the case of modern wellbores, it's brand new casing, brand new pipe, and brand new cement. It's not going to fail if installed correctly.

There have been more than a million wells drilled in the United States, and it's almost unheard of to have failure high enough where it would contaminate the potable water table. Again, the last thing any operator wants to do is go cheap and risk that. Also, there are regulations on how wellbores are constructed. Once the hole is drilled, you put the casing down it and then cement around the outside of the casing. It's stronger than solid rock. It's steel casing with brand new hard concrete and then bedrock. Bedrock isn't as strong as steel.

When you frack it, the last thing that will fail is the steel casing. Then when you put fracks on further down the wellbore, that's still a revolution that's going on not just in unconventional reservoirs like shales and tight sands and that sort of thing, but even conventional reservoirs. It's like the pyramid of resources.

In some ways, the advent of successful fracking is analogous to the gold rush of days gone by. Years ago, people in pursuit of gold went out to find it by panning it out of the rivers. That gold rush played out long ago. Basically about 1860 to 1880 was the last time anything was found, and that was in Alaska. Those days ended so people started looking for not just plaster gold, but load gold. They went around in the mountains looking for certain coloration that indicated mineralization. Most of the time, there's nothing there. Once in a while, they found a little vein of gold and boomtowns popped up.

The last time that happened was the 1920s and the 30s, and then that was over. Starting in the 1950s and the 60s, people started looking for this really finely disseminated gold. It's two or three atoms of gold. You can't see them. In fact, it's called micron gold. Those deposits are out in Nevada and elsewhere, but mostly parts of Nevada, and those things are huge. Net present estimated value is $15 billion in some of those mines. They're huge resources. Over the span of their lives, they'll produce $50 to $60 billion worth of gold.

The point is it started with the highest grade, and over time it moved to the lowest grade but larger volumes. There will be larger volumes of low-grade product. That makes sense. It's like that with oil and gas. There's still a huge amount of oil and resources left, but now it's the poor quality resource, it's the tighter reservoirs. That's where fracking comes in. Whether it's traditional plays or unconventional, these new things have popped up in the last 20 years and fracking is the magic button.

But long before any drilling takes place, companies like Wright Drilling have a process for locating and then evaluating potential project areas, even before they are ever offered to investing partners. The first part of this process is called exploration.

Exploration

<u>Oil and Gas Exploration</u>

Oil = Energy = Prosperity

The oil and gas industry is vitally, crucially important to humanity as a whole. These two resources account for more than half of the world population's energy supply needs.

Energy production is necessary to support life at this point. With more than seven billion people living on the planet today, low-energy levels and agrarian ways of life are no longer possible. Billions would die of starvation without the oil and gas industry. Continued oil and gas production and exploration is imperative at this point in our existence.

Countries with the highest energy consumption, typically, provide the highest quality of life for their residents. Access to reliable energy is directly related to the economy of a given nation. New technology, advanced medical care, improved infrastructure, job creation, so many aspects of stability and growth can be directly attributed to increased power production and use.

Innovation leads to the demand for more power, and the ability to access it touches almost every part of our lives. Think outside the commercial, industrial and transportation needs and look inward. The country's residential sector contributes to the exponential

HYDROCARBON EXPLORATION

Hydrocarbon exploration (or oil and gas exploration) is the search by petroleum geologists and geophysicists for hydrocarbon deposits beneath the Earth's surface, such as oil and natural gas. Oil and gas exploration are grouped under the science of petroleum geology.

Visible surface features such as oil seeps, natural gas seeps, pockmarks (underwater craters caused by escaping gas) provide basic evidence of hydrocarbon generation (be it shallow or deep in the Earth). However, most exploration depends on highly sophisticated technology to detect and determine the extent of these deposits using exploration geophysics. When a prospect has been identified and evaluated and passes the oil company's selection criteria, an exploration well is drilled in an attempt to conclusively determine the presence or absence of oil or gas.

energy demand. In 2015 alone, the United States consumed more than 27 trillion cubic feet (Tcf) of natural gas, the majority of it going to electric power generation.

Natural gas has become a major player in the energy market, making up about 26 percent of the total energy consumption.

Imagine this: In the 1920s, fewer than 40 percent of American homes had access to electricity. In less than 20 years, just one generation later, nearly 100 percent of homes were wired for electric power. Think about the items contained in just about every home—refrigerator, water heater, stove, microwave, dishwasher, etc. A lot of power is needed to run these things.

Some may argue regulations requiring appliances to be made to operate more efficiently than they did in the past would help to reduce the need for more residential power. However, most likely any gains made by this are offset by the sheer number of electronics and appliances owned by a typical American household, a number that continually grows as these items become more available and inexpensive. Today, half of all homes in the U.S. own three or more television sets, most own at least one personal computer and rechargeable device (cell phone, tablet, etc.), and more than 65 percent use central heating and air conditioning.

Now consider energy needs of a larger scale. Entire trade sectors have been designed around oil and gas and without it, those industries involved would fail. The transportation industry, for example, is wholly dependent on oil and gas to power it: airlines, ships and trucks. If you think about it, almost everything you possess was at some point transported by something fueled by oil or natural gas before coming into your possession. Interestingly, petroleum is the most common power source fueling the transportation industry. At the same time, petroleum accounts for a massive portion of the transportation business. Almost half of all cargo being transported across our oceans, rivers, and waterways is petroleum.

Industrial needs also play a role in the supply and demand of natural gas. This fuel is used often in the agriculture and pharmaceutical industries and power plants.

Over the course of 150 years or so, we, as a global population, have conditioned our lives around oil and gas products. Oil is huge and it is not going away. New advances make promises about being the "answer" to oil, but realistically, no viable replacements for it exist. And this will most likely remain the case throughout our lifetimes. Alternative sources of energy are making strides, but in actual production, they do not even make a dent in meeting our energy demands. Imagine the scale in which we use petroleum today…the sheer numbers of cars, trucks, machines, military equipment, ships, planes. Displacing it with new technology will not only be an undertaking on an astronomical scale, but would also require unimaginable amounts of dollars to fund it.

It All Starts With a Project

Oil and gas ventures are capital-intensive. Each project, from concept to completion, is a highly involved team effort.

Exploring for oil and natural gas involves professional leaders from many career fields. Wright Drilling has developed strategic partnerships and created an expert team with more than half a century of combined experience among oil and gas professionals from a multitude of vocations across the industry. From geologists, operators, and land men, to banking, legal, and insurance representatives, our comprehensive team has all bases covered.

We operate as an independent energy drilling and exploration company, primarily engaging in crude oil and natural gas development and production. Our projects are located in states that are among the highest in the country in regards to oil and gas production yields, and we strive to diversify our company projects geographically and geologically. In addition to Oklahoma and Texas, we also have working interest, plans, or prospects in Louisiana and, with our most recent endeavor in Kansas.

The basic steps an oil and natural gas company follows for most exploration projects are: researching probable oil-containing areas, making contact with mineral owners, securing a lease, further research, and finally, drilling a well.

Our team analyzes all potential oil and gas deals and acquisitions with a data-driven decision-making process, considering all aspects of every stage of exploration and development before making a commitment.

We consider the past and current performance of wells in a selected area and study drilling activity trends for all prospects under our review. We work to identify any vulnerability or potential hazard that may arise, and then work through a plan to manage, minimize and eliminate the risks. If we cannot work through and find solutions for any issues discovered, we do not pursue the project.

Unlike many other oil and gas investment companies, we invest our own money into all ventures we assume. We protect the financial stakes of our partners with the same fervor with which we look after our own. When you make an investment with Wright Drilling, we want you to take comfort knowing we are in this together from the inception of the project and throughout. And, we turn around and reinvest our profits back into the company to fund more developing projects.

Loma Linda #1

Wright Drilling funded its first project before the business's planning book was even put together. This is uncommon in this industry, but we did it and it was funded based on trust and because of the relationships I had with the people brought on board. I heard, "Get me the paperwork when you can, Mike," as they wrote me a check.

That's a good feeling. It all comes down to quality business principles.

I've seen other oil and gas companies take up to two years to obtain the funding and get their first project off the ground. I think it speaks volumes that Wright Drilling was able to fund our first well so quickly.

From onset to drilling our first well, which was successful, less than 60 days had elapsed.

This first project was drilling a well in Okfuskee County, Oklahoma, called the Loma Linda #1. A drilling permit on a 200-acre oil lease was going to expire soon, and the company that owned the lease did not have the capital to drill it. So we stepped in. Instead of allowing the permit to expire, Wright Drilling and C&C Productions partnered to make it happen by buying out the lease and quickly going to work.

We began construction at the site in late March 2016, and spudded the well on April 9. (Spudding means the process of beginning to drill a well.) We hit the project's total depth (TD) target of approximately 3,800 feet within five days. Log evaluations and core samples taken from the bore hole confirmed the presence of multiple hydrocarbon-bearing zones beneath the surface.

We'd struck oil.

Hydrocarbon is a term you will see often in this book, and hear often in this industry. It refers to an organic compound that consists of only hydrogen and carbon atoms. Hydrocarbon comes in several varieties and is found in many places. For our purposes, they are found in both natural gas and crude oil.

Based on geological surveys, soil sampling, and the history of other producing wells in the area, we predict this Oklahoma well will have long-lasting production of recoverable oil and natural gas, which means solid returns for our partners and ourselves.

The Loma Linda #1 is an offset well, which means it is near an existing proven and producing well. No wildcatting—drilling in unproven areas—was involved. By drilling in areas with confirmed production, we minimize our risks.

It is a very successful site at this point because we have four layers of the earth—what we call four "k-zones" of oil—to go into and take out of those reserves. As we write this book in the summer of 2016, we are in the fracking phase of that well. We will discuss fracking in much greater detail later in the book. After fracking, we'll put the pump jack on the well and start pumping out the oil. As the book was being written in mid-2016, we were also in the process of having additional wells permitted for drilling on this lease.

It's very important to note I learned of this opportunity because of surrounding myself with professionals in this industry. My geologist found that project. Then he showed me exactly why he thought we should drill there. I listened to what he said, ran it by a few other professional folks, and it all made perfect sense. We went out there and drilled, and we found four layers of the earth that produce oil. The professionals are the ones that helped us make that decision.

Key People Involved in a Project

Oil and gas deals typically involve the same three entities sharing the revenues made from producing wells: the mineral rights owner, the operator/project manager, and the group financing the cost of developing the well.

At the initial stage of a project, the specializations of the people involved will depend on whether the project site is previously drilled or not drilled. In the case of an undrilled field, geologists and geoscientists will do most of the initial analysis. For a previously drilled field, engineers will analyze what is known about the site to determine its future viability.

Geologist at Work

A geologist, who may work independently or under contract of one of the entities involved, will conduct research in areas of known or probable oil and gas resources. The first thing the geologist will do is look at an area that has some production around it, and he or she will pursue two-dimensional, or "2D," seismic data through the use of reflection seismology. (See illustration, next page.)

Reflection seismology is a method of exploration geophysics that uses the principles of seismology to estimate the properties of the Earth's subsurface from reflected seismic waves. It requires a controlled seismic source of energy such as dynamite or a specialized air gun or seismic vibrator. Reflection seismology is similar to sonar. Two-dimensional (2D)seismic data is obtained through a seismic survey engineered for the most efficiency in terms of cost and time. It's a way to, in effect, take a peek at what's under the surface. If you like what you see in a 2D survey, then you may move to a three-dimensional (3D) survey. Two-dimensional data provides only a cross section of what you would see in a 3D survey.

Two-dimensional seismic data is obtained when you set off a charge. The energy goes down through the earth and reflects off layers of rock below. It's like when you're inside a building—the materials in the walls, ceilings and floors influence the levels of reflectivity of light and sound that come off those surfaces. We've all been in houses where everything is marble, and it's more reflective—sound waves, in particular. If you're in a house with drywall and it has a little texture on it, it's not nearly as reflective. The sound waves don't reverberate as much, and the light waves don't reflect as much.

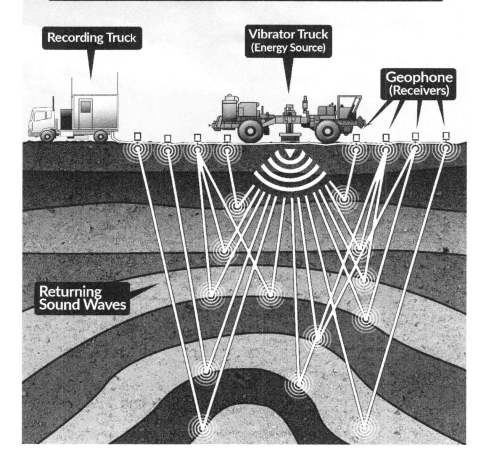

The same thing happens with rocks and subsurface. When the energy waves generated by dynamite or a specialized tool hit those subsurface interfaces, they reflect. Some of the energy keeps going past one particular interface, and some of it reflects back. As it keeps going, it'll reflect off the next layer that has good acoustic contrast.

Once the charge is set off, the resulting wave reflections occur in a matter of seconds. Most of what you're interested in is reflected within the first two to three seconds. For something that's really deep, you might have data that comes back in four seconds.

The reflecting waves are vibrations of such low frequency the human ear can't pick them up. So they are measured by specialized equipment, including devices similar to the seismograph you see measuring the strength of earthquakes.

In the oil expiration business, all of the data is recorded on computer-filled trucks and then goes to seismic processing. It's a substantial process that gives you a picture of the subsurface.

Land surveys, soil samples, maps, and 2D and 3D seismic reports and magnetic readings are a few of the methods a geologist uses to determine if an area has the potential to produce oil. Using these advanced and highly precise techniques, they measure depths and types of rocks along with their porosity and permeability. With this information, geologists are able to give a nearly accurate calculation of whether a location likely contains oil or not. Ultimately though, there is no way to be certain without drilling.

"Virgin fields" (ones that have not yet been drilled) are much higher risk than fields which have already been drilled because your chances are a whole lot better of finding no hydrocarbons than finding a brand new productive field. On the other hand, if you find hydrocarbons, that field has a high probability of being very, very lucrative.

The Role of Engineers

On the other hand, when you're in an old field that's been picked around for the last 50 years, you'll probably find something that tempts you to complete the well, or maybe not. Even if it looks good to where you complete it, the biggest risk is its level of depletion. Am I drilling in an area where I can't actually get more money back than I just put in because it's been depleted? It's an important question to answer for existing fields.

When that very field was first discovered 50 years earlier, that wouldn't have been a question. That well wasn't going to be just economic, but lucrative, too. Fifty years later, the depletion question—what is still left there—is what we're up against. It's lower risk than a virgin field because chances are you'll find something. The chances are probably 50 percent to make a profitable return on the well.

Therefore, engineers come into play in fields which have already been discovered and/or drilled. The field may be available for additional exploration for any number of reasons. It is the engineers who read the data and history of the field to come up with data and recommendations on whether or not to start a new project on this partially-depleted field.

Mineral Owners

Before any drilling can commence, though, the people who own the land are brought into the process. The owners of the surface and mineral rights, called "fee interest," of a plot of land to be explored for oil are key figures in the negotiations for the prospective oil and gas lease. Mineral owners enter into this type of an agreement to permit oil and gas operations to be conducted on their property, bearing no responsibility for costs associated with drilling and operations. In exchange, they receive a royalty interest in the well.

Royalty interests are a negotiated percentage rate of the gross production revenue of successful wells drilled on a specific property and paid to the mineral owner. Royalty amounts vary, but one-eighth to one-fourth of the production is typical throughout the industry.

The details of the agreements are negotiated between a project manager's representative called a land man, and a mineral rights owner. They are captured in a legally binding oil, gas, and mineral lease contract.

Most leases offer an up-front bonus to mineral owners, typically based on a price per acre, and the specifics of the royalty percentage promised, as well as the planned timing or price benchmarks for royalty statements and payouts. Royalty values are based on many variables including the geology of the land, size of the acreage, and whether the existence of hydrocarbons is known, unknown, or considered highly likely.

Similar to investors looking to participate in partnerships, it is in the mineral rights owner's best interest to perform due diligence prior to entering into any agreements or contracts concerning oil and gas exploration on their land. One way is by researching producing wells within a close vicinity to their property to gain an understanding of possible expectations.

For a mineral owner with multiple plots of land, one of the best strategies to ensure maximum income potential and avoid issues that may arise with multiple projects is to insist on separate contracts for each plot of land.

Land owners are also compensated for surface use of the land and damages that may occur during drilling and completions. The timeline from start to finish usually ranges from a few weeks to as many as 90 days.

Operations Team Starts Drilling

An operations team, which includes a drilling engineer, will perform the next phase of exploration by drilling. Based on the findings and input from the geologist, the team will set up and drill a test well in an effort to tap into an underground reservoir of oil or gas. An experienced engineer can determine the proper location, equipment needed, and the best course necessary for access.

Often, investment groups participate in these types of oil-drilling projects. Companies acting in this capacity typically have a working interest in the well and represent the financial interests of multiple entities who provide the capital needed to fund a project in exchange for returns from production earnings.

Once a well begins producing, any yields from the rig are measured on-site. This measurement is what shares are based upon when calculating payout. Cash prices for oil produced from a well are set monthly. Royalty payments are subject to taxation as ordinary income and, other than percentage depletion allowances, are not permitted the generous tax shelter and allowances available to operators and partners of oil and gas projects. The tax advantages for general and limited partners are detailed later in the book.

Drilling Rigs and Components

Building a drilling rig from the ground up takes many people and companies, as well as each individual's hard work and dedication to safety and excellence. Detailed plans, permits, secure financial backing and profuse amounts of research are required. (See the illustration on the next page for the components of a drilling rig.)

Before the decision to drill is finalized, there are a number of steps. Everybody on the team huddles around the proposal and throws a thousand questions at it. Early on, most of the questions are geoscience-oriented, such as, "How close is the nearest spot of

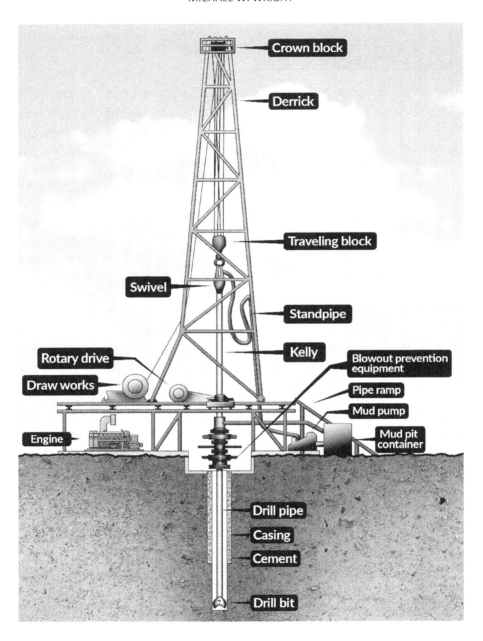

production? What do those wells produce? What is the thermal maturity of the source rocks (that generate the oil and gas) in this area?"

There are a thousand questions that need answers. Most of them are obvious, but they still need to be answered to ensure the process is thorough. Let's say the prospective project is a few miles from a field that previously produced hydrocarbons. If that field had source rock that generated oil and charged that field, things are not going to change so quickly over two miles to where all of a sudden it's bad—unless you knew for some reason the source rock shale pinched out or something between the two areas.

That source field reservoir is analyzed. Then, the project gets handed from the geoscientists to a petroleum engineer. At this point, the key questions include: "Where is the nearest pipeline?" Or, "If it's oil, where do we truck it?" These questions must be answered to determine if the project will be economically feasible.

If it's a natural gas project, you can't truck gas. That means a pipeline must be used to transport it. A gas-gathering line will need to be set up to take it to some major gas pipeline. How far away is the existing pipeline? How much will it cost to get this gathering line to that major pipeline? What's the pipeline company going to charge for a tap into its line? What are they going to charge me to carry my gas to market?

The gas pipeline company is trying to make profit on the pipeline. If you've got something to deliver, that's great for them. In a perfect world, it's great for everyone to make money together. If they didn't have that pipe there, then you'd have to lay it. A lot of little fields wouldn't be economically viable to produce profit when it costs $2 billion to lay the pipe. There's just no way.

Let's say you make $2.50 per MCF (thousand cubic feet of natural gas), and the pipeline company wants something like $0.25 per MCF to carry your gas to market, or 10 percent. If they weren't there, you'd be out of business because you couldn't afford to go spend billions of dollars for some little tiny field you just found. But the pipeline company bridges that gap. It's a win-win for everybody.

Oil is easier to transport, and here's why. Each tanker truck is actually a little piece of oil pipeline sitting on wheels. That little piece of pipeline can come and pick up oil from the tank farm, and then that little segment of pipeline on wheels will take it to the refinery. I'm saying that somewhat jokingly, but little segments of pipeline are one way to look at a tanker truck fleet.

Oil can be carried that way easily, whereas if you tried to carry gas, the amount of gas value that would fill a truck is not worth trucking. It's about $30 worth of natural gas, or methane, that you can pump into a tanker before it fills up. If you're taking $30 worth of product to market and it costs $100 for the round trip, it just doesn't make any financial sense.

That's why with gas you need pipelines to get it there economically. In this day and age, there are trains and trucks that will compress gas and liquefy it. But, to set up those kinds of apparatus to liquefy methane and put it on trucks, again, is not economic. It makes no sense. Pipeline wins every time.

On shore, it's never made sense to go through all that trouble to liquefy it just to put it on trucks and transport it. When they're doing that for offshore-type markets like in Indonesia, they have big gas fields there. They liquefy it and carry it on large barges to Japan. Again, there's a scale and enough volume there for it to make sense financially.

You can move oil through pipelines as well, and that is always the preference if it is economical. When it isn't, you can still afford to transport oil to market over a span of a couple hundred miles by tanker truck. Say oil is selling for $50 a barrel and it costs you $8 a barrel to transport it by truck. You can just buy your own truck and do it yourself. When it costs you $8 a barrel to transport it and you get $50 a barrel for it at the refinery, you make $42 a barrel. It works.

Another big consideration in deciding whether or not to drill is the quantity of oil and gas reserves. How much is there? What's the upside potential, and what's the expected value of hydrocarbon reserves? How much is there?

What will be the initial production rate? If it has a billion barrels in it, that sounds great on the surface. But if the rock is so tight and lacking permeability that the most you can get out of it at any one time is a barrel a day, that's not economic.

The rate is just as important as the volume. Would I rather have a 10-million-barrel field producing all 10 million barrels in a year, or would I rather have a 20-million-barrel field producing it in 100 years? I'd rather get the 10 million barrels in a year than the 20 million in 100 years.

Those are extreme examples, but the bottom line is we want the most reserves possible and the highest production rates possible. The reserves are the ultimate factor of whether this project has value. If it has value, then the production rate comes into play. Every well needs to yield a certain number of barrels a day just to break even on all the costs that went into it, such as the lease, operating expense, etc.

Pressure Depletion vs. Water-Driven Reservoirs

Whatever that number is, then you have to count in depletion. If it is a depletion reservoir, the rate will diminish over time.

Let's say the field started off at 7,000 pounds per square inch of pressure in the reservoir. Then you drilled into it and, some way or another, the reservoir is "bounded"—like a balloon surrounding it. The balloon has boundaries. When you put a straw in that balloon, you pull the gas out. The subsurface around it doesn't shrink, but the balloon shrinks.

When a balloon shrinks, the pressure decreases as you pull the gas out of the balloon. The expanded rubber around the balloon will actually give you some energy—the elastic strain energy put in there when you put the gas in the balloon. When you let the pressure out and the gas out, the pressure reduces.

In the subsurface, it's even more exaggerated than that, because it's not a balloon that can keep up and follow you. When you pull gas out, you reduce the pressure in the reservoir in the subsurface. Over the span of time in a pressure-depletion reservoir, there's less and less and less gas down there to produce, and it has less and less pressure over the span of time to actually have energy to get the gas out. There's only so much gas in there and it's bounded. It doesn't just keep going forever.

On the other hand, water-drive reservoirs are steady because water keeps moving in on it. That water acts like the skin of the balloon. The water keeps pushing that oil and gas upward. In an exceptional water-drive reservoir, you have virtually no reduction in reservoir pressure as you produce it.

A pressure release depletion reservoir is a bounded reservoir that comes down to an issue of scales. On this end of the scale, you're definitely going to reduce the pressure in the reservoir. Water-drive reservoirs are the other kind, the other end of the scale. Everywhere you have an oil or gas field, there's always oil or gas sitting on top of water. It will either be gas on oil and water, oil on water, or gas on water. Water will flow into the reservoir to take the place of the oil and/or gas being extracted, maintaining the pressure, by and large.

Think about when you try to mix oil and water. The oil always rises to the top. And of course, any gas will rise above water. The same is true underground.

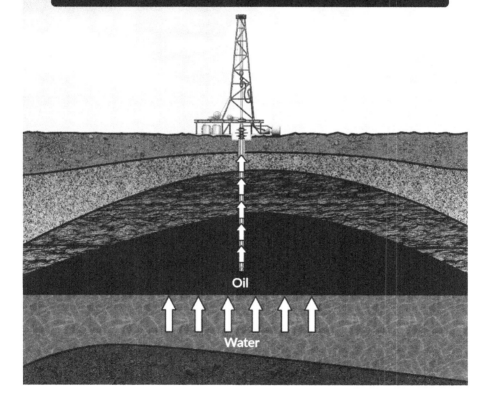

Most reservoirs lean one way or the other. There are very few pure pressure depletion or pure water-driven reservoirs. Really tight reservoirs tend to be pressure depletion. Really, really porous ones tend to be water-pressure driven.

The Land Man

Even if all of the above look positive, nothing can happen until you actually have the rights to drill on the land. Enter the land person, known commonly as the "land man." While the subsurface and transportation analyses are going on, the land man helps you answer questions like: How much does it cost? What's the history of this area? Is it federal acreage? Is it privately held acreage? Has the land owner ever wanted a lease before? Is the reason this prospect field is still here is because the person has never wanted to grant a lease? Some people just flat don't like money, which is a real problem when you run into people like that.

But you can also find situations like the one above in which a generation or two later, the heirs like money more than grandpa and grandma. One of the land man's jobs is to check and not assume anything based on previous history.

The land man is also very important because the only face your lessor—the person who owns minerals out there, whether it's the federal government or a private citizen—sees most of the time is the land man. They don't see the geophysicist. They don't see the geologist. They don't see the petroleum engineer. The face of your company to the people on whose land you are operating is the land man.

It's very important that the land man be good with people. He also needs to be sharp about keeping track of things—not necessarily with numbers, but maps, land and just staying on top of accounts. We might opt to hire a land man who works locally in the area in which we are exploring. This puts a local face on the deal. We can hire them on a day rate, the same way we would hire a consulting geophysicist or consulting geologist or consulting petroleum engineer.

The land man can tell you early on whether there are obstacles in a region for any reason. He can save you a lot of time that you might otherwise waste if you consider a field which might be federally protected or unavailable for another reason.

Safety is first and foremost at our drill sites, as should be the case at all sites. Finding oil and natural gas is the ultimate end goal of any drilling project, but reaching that goal safely is the absolute priority.

Before you can drill a rig, all the proper permits and lease agreements need to be approved and readily available. From onset, operations at a rig typically go on 24 hours a day by crews working in 12 hours shifts.

Get Quotes on the Drilling Job

One of the first steps is to bid out the job of developing the drilling rig. For the best combination of a reasonable price and knowing your contractor is reputable and reliable, it's a good idea to get bids from three to five different rig drilling firms.

You wouldn't want to hire someone and then find out they don't know what they're doing. If you had a budget of say $500,000 and the contractor blows through $400,000 quickly, you might have a hole that's non-functional because the driller screwed it up for you. You want somebody who really knows what they're doing on the drilling end of things.

All of the expenses of the project up to this point have been cheap by comparison. The seismic tests are cheap. The land rights are cheap. Drilling is when the big dollars are spent. That's the make or break of any prospect site.

If there was a way with geology for geophysics and engineering to know exactly what you're going to find on some newly generated prospect without drilling a well, you'd just sell the reserves to somebody. For example, you might know you have two million barrels in the reservoir. It's worth $40 a barrel. You might sell it to someone for $30 a barrel, and you didn't even have to drill a well. However, the reason you must drill a well before selling your reserves is it is still the only way to absolutely know whether there's nothing or something down there. The process is very expensive, so you want to make sure you have a good drilling company.

It's easy to check them out. You ask them who they have drilled wells for previously, and then you reach out in the industry for references. And, you don't just call the references the potential contractor provided. You call around to others in the industry to see what they have experienced and heard.

There are different ways you can contract drilling. You can do it by the subterranean foot, at a day rate, or even "turnkey." A lot of people like turnkey contracts. Let's say a well will cost $1 million to drill. On a turnkey contract, you might pay $1.15 million. You knowingly pay $150,000 more for the same wellbore. What you get for that $150,000 is the contractor's assurance they're going to get that well done. In a turnkey contract, the drilling company guarantees the job will be done correctly, even if there are unforeseen circumstances or accidents along the way. The drilling company absorbs any additional costs as part of the contract, meaning a company like ours can budget with a much greater certainty of accuracy. In effect, the premium price of a turnkey contract represents an insurance policy purchased by the project manager.

A good drilling company operator will offer a turnkey deal, provided it's not a high-risk drilling area. On the other hand, a turnkey contract isn't worth the paper it's written on if whoever offers it is a crook. About 95 percent of the time, things run the way everybody expects them to. It's that 5 percent of the time when issues happen.

Here's how a day-rate contract functions differently: a day rate is the amount a drilling contractor gets paid by the oil company for a day of operating a drilling rig. The companies and the contractors usually agree on a flat fee per contract, so the day rate is determined by dividing the total amount by the number of days in the contract.

And here is a scenario in which a project manager may opt for a day-rate contract: Let's say your prospect reservoir is 6,000 feet below the surface, and your drilling company has reached 4,000 feet total depth. You still have 2,000 feet to go to get down to your objective to test it. It's a well that has already cost you more than a million dollars, but you're still expecting that additional distance.

You're already at $1.5 million spent and over budget. All your partners are wondering what's going on. You're having all kinds of hole problems. At that point, all of the key partners in the project get together for a come-to-Jesus meeting to decide what the next steps will be. Some people might want to just keep going, and other people might drop out. There are clauses in standard contracts that allow any partner or investor an "out" on a project having major hole problems.

For all the partners who stay, it's theirs. If they find a big oil field, it's theirs. Sometimes the way the contract is written, people who opt out can get back in, but only after the well has paid out something like more than three times the cost. It would have to be one hell of a well to actually pay out three times over cost, and then still have something left to make the person who opted out anxious to get back in. Usually by then, unless it's something like the East Texas Oil Field, there won't be much left there after it's produced enough to pay out 300 percent of the cost.

A day rate contract is preferable in this case because you have a wellbore already over budget and fraught with problems. If you run into even more problems, and the group decides at some future point the project needs to be abandoned, you won't pay any more to a drilling contractor than for the work that company performs.

Building a Rig

Before a crew can actually build a rig, it must first gain access to the property. Many times, drilling relocations are in remote, unimproved areas that must undergo a transformation in order to be called a proper drill site. Building a road to gain access to the location is, in most cases, the first step.

Next, the area is cleared, strengthened and leveled in preparation for the new rig and all the dozens of flat-bed semis loaded with drilling equipment and supplies that will soon fill the area. Once this is completed, the area can begin preparation for water and power at the drill site by building the infrastructure needed to support it.

A few holes will likely need to be dug around the rig, one example being a large dirt (sometimes lined) pit which will serve to avert surface or water table pollution during the drilling process. The water table is important when considering the depth of a well, with the target typically falling no closer than 50 to 75 feet below the water table. Great care must be exercised to ensure the water table is protected during the entire drilling process.

The depth of the target location determines the size and complexity of the rig; the deeper the hole being drilled, the larger the rig. For our purposes, thus far, with drilling 5,000 feet or less, the rig can be assembled by a team of approximately 15 to 20 crew members and be ready for inspection in two to three days.

Once the rig has passed inspection, drilling can commence. Drilling is done in three phases: drilling, casing and tubing.

First, the casing is prepared and a wide conductor hole is bored, usually a few hundred feet deep, stopping just below the water table. Casing pipe is installed and cemented in place in order to protect the groundwater and surrounding soil from contamination, as well as to help stabilize the wellbore. The well is then drilled to the targeted total depth, reaching the intended pay zone.

Before drilling can begin, however, a key safety feature, a blowout preventer, must be installed on the casing head. A blowout preventer is equipped with high-pressure safety valves that prevent blowouts by sealing off and blocking any escaping oil or gas. (See illustration, next page.) Mud may be pumped into the drill stem, but flow back up and out is prevented.

Many things can happen during either stage of drilling that may temporarily halt operations. One possibility is "tripping out" the drill bit if it breaks or gets worn down by drilling. The terrain determines the life of a drill bit and harder ground can shorten that life. The tripping out process is quite involved and usually shuts down drilling for several hours as it requires the cooling of the bit and the removal of the entire string of pipe. Close monitoring is needed to ensure the hole remains intact during this time.

Mud is used in drilling to help cool the drill bit, maintain pressure within the well, and help clear out cuttings created by the drill bit. Mud pumped into the well and mud system equipment (to remove sand, gas and silt) are used to separate the chunks of ground-up earth from drilling and also keep the hole from becoming plugged. The mud from the hole is sent through a shaker to separate the cuttings, and then clean mud is recirculated down the hole.

Sections of pipe are added periodically as the drilling goes deeper until the targeted TD is reached. Mud readings can be taken throughout the drilling process from cuttings to give an estimation

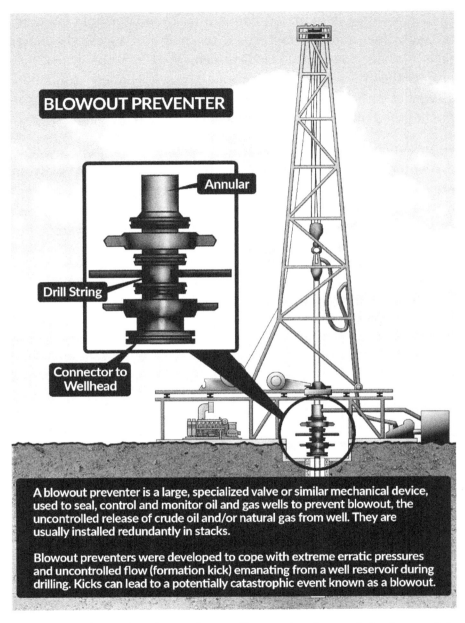

of hydrocarbons levels in the wellbore. At that point, the well is flushed and conditioned in preparation for logging, which provides a wealth of information about the state of the well. With this information, a company can determine whether the well is a viable source for producing oil or gas.

A mud logger, usually with a geologic background and some training in geoscience, is part of the crew at this stage. Some of the best mud loggers in the world were self-taught right in the oil field. They look at samples that drift up through the water and mud. They're as good as a Ph.D. in geoscience, because that's all they've ever done. They're smart, and they get very good at their specialty.

Rock chips are cut from the formation by the drill bit, and brought to the surface with the mud. They are used by the mud logger to obtain formation data. The mud logger looks at the rock chips under a microscope, utilizing chemicals that you can put on them under fluorescent light. That "cut" can be an early indication of how good the well will be. The analysis provides early information on the porosity of the underground rock.

On the other hand, if the drilling has reached the depth of your reservoir, you might not see any cut at all. But you keep drilling. You hope you're getting ready to drill into something that's suddenly just 100 percent oil saturation, which can rarely happen. But usually it's about 70 percent oil saturation and 30 percent water.

The only places that have ever really had 100 percent water cut are places like California, where so much oil moves through some of those reservoirs, they're literally flushed in the water that was in those sandstones. There was 100 percent water in them before the oil came in. Then, so much oil went through the sandstone it literally pushed all the water out. It's an extremely rare circumstance, but it can happen.

Your mud logger continues looking at samples under the microscope. He or she keeps putting chemicals on the samples, looking for cut. Every day, sometimes twice a day, reports are sent to the drilling operator, who in turn sends reports to the partners.

Everybody's hopeful for good signs, but it is what it is. This is all part of the process known as formation evaluation we touched on earlier in the book. As often as possible, you are looking for signs that signal what, if anything, is likely to come from the reservoir you have targeted and are drilling into. But we don't put all our faith in just a sample part of the formation evaluation, because it doesn't show everything.

At the end of it all, you want to run logs that you can look at. That's a key part of the formation evaluation. What happens in this exploratory mode is you've drilled down through the reservoir, and you run your logs. When you have a log showing promising signs, you can then go down the wellbore with a sidewall core or even a percussive core, which shoots off a shotgun-type shell and take rock samples.

This is how to obtain larger, bigger, more representative pieces of that reservoir than you would see from just those cutting samples— little sawed-off pieces coming up with the mud. Now you get a better look at it. You can analyze it for oil saturation, that sort of thing. Obviously, it works better with an oil reservoir than a gas or methane reservoir.

You send it off to a core lab which can run a quick core description of it. At this point, you can often tell the depth of your reservoir that will yield hydrocarbons. For example, you may have expected a 30-foot depth of reservoir to yield product, but maybe you determine that only 15 of those 30 will actually produce gas or oil. You run the numbers on it, and you can determine if it will be economical.

Even if it won't be profitable, there are still occasions when you might continue drilling. You never want an unprofitable well, but an important consideration is all the costs already in it. As you're looking at the analytical data, you might say, "Well, we think there's about $400,000 worth of oil there. Nothing to write home about, but it will only cost us $100,000 to complete it."

For $100,000 expenditure now, all our costs up to this point are water under the bridge. You won't make a profit, but you will reclaim some of those sunk costs. If the well costs a million bucks, I'm losing money—but not as much as I would have. I'll recover $300,000 by producing the well.

There's an expression in the oil industry that you don't want to encounter a "teaser" in the formation evaluation. You completed the well because it looked like it was either fully economic, or it looked like you were going to make profit at least on the completion—so it teased you along and you took the bait. Once the well is completed, you expected 50 barrels a day and, in actuality, it only yields five barrels a day.

Your initial rate is puny compared to what you thought. It's definitely not economic. You produce it for a month just to be sure, or four months, but you're losing money every month. You keep diddling with it. You keep rethinking it. You talk to different engineers. But at some point, you realize you got teased.

Well Stimulation

Hydraulic fracturing, or fracking—to stimulate and/or increase the flow of hydrocarbons from the well—has become a common part of domestic drilling. This two-to-three-day process in which water, sand, and chemicals are injected deep into the ground at high pressure create and hold open small cracks in the rocks to allow the release of trapped oil and gas. This process maximizes extraction possibilities of underground resources. Fracking has enabled drilling and extraction in areas previously thought too cost-prohibitive for wells in the past, including unusual reservoirs in shale, coal, and tight sand. Most shale reserves would remain undeveloped and untapped if fracking was not available.

Fracking a well requires many permits and adherence to many local, state and federal regulations and guidelines. Four areas of fracking operations most often addressed regarding regulations and permits are pre-drilling planning, groundwater and surface water impact, liquid wastes and fluids, and solid wastes. Water management plans are required to identify the sources used, amounts required, and any anticipated environmental impact that may result. Fluid and solid waste disposal plans disclose locations where "flowback," or waste water, and drilling mud or cuttings will be stored, treated and disposed following a frack. Site safety plans and any waivers requested are also part of the process.

Up front, fracking a well can be an expensive and highly involved process, but the payoffs in production and profitability can be incredible.

Also, fracking is a method that may be used later on should the well begin under producing, or on a well which has been out of production. Many fields thought exhausted and abandoned are actually still able to produce millions of gallons. Old wells can be "reworked" using new technology and at a much lower cost than drilling new wells. Additional options include well work-overs (major maintenance), acid washing and flushing with drilling fluids to rouse a well back to optimal production.

As mentioned earlier in the book, the combination of fracking and directional and/or horizontal drilling has been revolutionary and led to a boom in the domestic oil and gas industry. Directional wells are those that deviate from the vertical drilling position. Those drilled completely perpendicular are called horizontal wells. Horizontal wells, which jut out in one or more directions from the vertical borehole once the tight rock and shale formations have been reached, permit the recovery of vast amounts of oil and especially natural gas. Drilling wells that diverge in this way have made oil production possible in areas where the surface typically would not have been able to support drilling.

Cluster wells have also changed the landscape of drilling. In the past, multiple well pads would be constructed in order to access all the resources of an area. But, over the past decade, cluster wells, a single rig that supports multiple wells and maximizes exposure across the pay zone, have become common.

A transition is underway from typical drilling methods in favor of these new techniques, considering more than 90 percent of all oil and natural wells brought in over the past 20 years have done so by applying one or more of these advancements.

As you have read in this chapter, well drilling is full of key points at which the fate of a project can pivot. And data can sometimes serve as a "teaser," which sets producers up for disappointment. At the end of the day, you have to remember there have been billions and billions and billions of dollars made off of the production of hydrocarbons. There will be billions and billions and billions more made. It's just that it's not guaranteed. You need the right team, the right people. The process has many little nuances to it.

Completion or Abandonment?

If the well is deemed viable, it is readied for the completion process; if it turns out to be a "dry hole," it will be plugged and abandoned. Sophisticated logging procedures also provide engineers and operators the information needed to generate fracking plans.

A well determined to be a producing well must first be retested before completion procedures can take place. This involves reinserting the drill pipe the full depth of the well to certify it is still intact and then recirculate mud throughout.

In the last phase of drilling, the drill pipe is removed and production casing string is run the depth of the well and cemented in place. Small tubing, which will channel the flow of oil or gas throughout the well, is inserted into the hole. A perforation gun is then lowered to slightly below the targeted level and fired, causing a string of charges to create perforations in the casing. This connects the well to the reservoir source and allows the oil and/or gas to then enter the well.

The flow of the oil or gas will determine the location of a choke to control the movement of the hydrocarbons up the tubing and out of the well.

After the wellbore is sealed to prevent contamination, the rig is disassembled and removed. Now, a new crew can step in to wrap up the well completion by removing the blowout preventer and installing the production wellhead or pump jack.

Now it's time to start producing oil and making money.

Be a Healthy Skeptic

When someone comes to you with a project, always remember they like it because it's theirs. They would love to see a well get drilled into the field they discovered. Even if it only has a one in a thousand chance, it's a one in a thousand chance that their discovery can make money for them. If it does work, they'll end up being rich. They have a huge incentive.

Everybody is hunky dory about their own project. But as the investor, remember just because some geoscientist brought you something doesn't mean it's something good.

People proposing a project will often exaggerate the possibility of success. Not because they are being blatantly dishonest—more due to the fact they are very hopeful and optimistic. If a project has an actual one-in-ten chance of success, you might hear that enhanced to a one-in-three chance. Hope sizes how they represent it. As the investor, you have hope too, but you want to look at all these different opportunities and go with the one that feels right for you.

PUMPJACKS AND TANK BATTERIES

A pumpjack is the overground drive for a reciprocating piston pump in an oil well.

It is used to mechanically lift liquid out of the well if not enough bottom hole pressure exists for the liquid to flow all the way to the surface. The arrangement is commonly used for onshore wells producing little oil. Pumpjacks are common in oil-rich areas.

Often the liquid pumped out is an emulsion of crude oil and water. Pump size is also determined by the depth and weight of the oil to remove, with deeper extraction requiring more power to move the increased weight of the discharge column (discharge head).

A pumpjack converts the rotary motion of the motor to a vertical reciprocating motion to drive the pump shaft, and is exhibited in the characteristic nodding motion. The engineering term for this type of mechanism is a walking beam. It was often employed in stationary and marine steam engine designs in the 18th and 19th centuries.

A tank battery is a group of tanks that are connected to receive crude oil production from a well or a producing lease. A tank battery is also called a battery. In the tank battery, the oil volume is measured and tested before pumping the oil into the pipeline system.

One that felt right for us was our very first project in early 2016.

Once Wright Drilling and companies like us pump the oil and gas out of the ground, it doesn't go straight to your heating system or your gas tank. It first has to be modified, and this is the point when the gas and oil are sent to a refinery.

Refining

Refining the Product

One of the last components of a well's completion phase is the installation of holding tanks. The size and number of tanks installed depends on the amount of oil and natural gas being pumped from the well. When the well begins producing, oil is pumped from the ground, filtered, then stored in the holding tanks located at surface level until it is transported via tanker trucks or pipeline to a refinery.

The vast network of pipelines crisscrossing the earth distributing crude oil, natural gas and refined material, is immense. In the U.S. alone, more than 300,000 miles of active crude oil, petroleum products, and natural gas pipelines exist.

Upon arrival at a refinery, the oil and/or natural gas is put through a distilling process to convert it into usable products. Crude oil, in its natural state when pumped from the ground, is not practical for many purposes and must be refined to transform it into a useable form.

The petroleum refining process is completed in three steps: Separation, Conversion, and Treatment.

Separation – In this phase, molecules in crude are separated according to weight through a process of atmospheric distillation. The "topping" process, as it is also called, is done in a tall, cylindrical vat and involves the oil being heated to a temperature up to 400

OIL REFINERY

An oil refinery, such as the one shown here, is an industrial plant that refines crude oil into petroleum products such as diesel, gasoline and heating oils. Oil refineries essentially serve as the second stage in the production process following the actual extraction by oil rigs. The first step in the refining process is distillation where crude oil is heated at extreme temperatures to separate the different hydrocarbons.

The crude oil components, once separated, can be sold to different industries for a broad range of purposes. Lubricants can be sold to industrial plants immediately after distillation, but other products require more refining before reaching the final user. Major refineries have the capacity to process hundreds of thousand barrels of crude oil a day.

Natural gas also undergoes a refining process before it is used by consumers.

degrees, which causes it to vaporize. The vapors rise to the top of the cylinder, while the heavier molecules, such as tar, remain at the bottom. The rising vapors condense into liquid form as they rise and cool and are collected from varying heights within the container. Medium density molecules left over will undergo another separation process to recover useful, middle distillates such as diesel fuel.

Conversion – Lighter-weight liquids are in the highest demand for petroleum based products. But not enough of the light petrol is produced naturally or during the first phase of refining, so additional steps must be taken. Heavier weighted molecules left over from the first step undergo a catalytic cracking process in excess of 500 degrees to convert it into two or more lighter molecules. The more involved this process becomes, the greater its cost. The majority of products derived from this process include gasoline and diesel fuel.

Treatment – This process uses high temperature and pressure to remove corrosive and polluting elements such as sulfur. This is done to improve air quality and reduce pollution from the burning of petroleum products. Hydrogen and sulfur combine to form hydrogen sulfide, which is then removed.

According to the U.S Energy Information Administration, Americans use an average of 19.4 million barrels of petroleum per day.

Petroleum typically has a distillate processing gain, meaning the refining output is greater in volume than the input. This is because of density changes, heavy molecules being broken down into smaller, lighter ones, during the refining process. On average, each 42-gallon barrel of oil creates approximately 45 to 46 gallons of refined, finished products. Gasoline and diesel fuel, as previously stated, are the primary products refined from crude oil—a typical 42-gallon barrel of oil can produce almost 20 gallons of gas and 12 gallons of diesel. During refining, automotive fuels also undergo additional treatments including alkylation and a process called catalytic reforming to increase octane levels.

Scientific and technological advances, since the early 1900s to today, encouraged the creation of thousands of new products that can be made from crude oil and natural gas. Many raw materials made from refined petroleum are products that have become part of our daily lives including rubber and plastic goods, pharmaceuticals, fertilizer, cleaning products, a range of lubricants and waxes, and much more. In fact, more than 6,000 products are made from petroleum!

What Products Come From Crude Oil?

Here is a list of the primary products refined from crude oil, and the percentage of any single gallon of crude which is used to create the sub-product:

42 percent: Gasoline, a transparent, petroleum-derived liquid used primarily as fuel in internal combustion engines. It consists mostly of organic compounds obtained by the fractional distillation of petroleum, enhanced with a variety of additives.

The characteristic of a particular gasoline blend to resist igniting too early (which causes knocking and reduces efficiency in reciprocating engines) is measured by its octane rating. Gasoline is produced in several grades of octane rating. Tetraethyllead and other lead compounds are no longer used in most areas to regulate and increase octane-rating, but many other additives are put into gasoline to improve its chemical stability, control corrosiveness and provide fuel system "cleaning," and determine performance characteristics under intended use. Sometimes, gasoline also contains ethanol as an alternative fuel, for economic or environmental reasons.

22 percent: Diesel fuel, in general is any liquid fuel used in diesel engines, whose fuel detonation takes place without a spark, as a result of compression of the inlet air mixture and then injection of fuel. The most common type of diesel fuel is a specific fractional distillate of petroleum fuel oil, but alternatives not derived from petroleum, such as biodiesel, biomass to liquid (BTL) or gas to liquid (GTL) diesel, are increasingly being developed and adopted. Diesel engines have found broad use as a result of higher thermodynamic and concurrent fuel efficiencies. This is particularly noted where diesel engines run at part-load; as their air supply is not throttled as in a petrol engine, their efficiency still remains very high.

9 percent: Jet fuel, aviation turbine fuel (ATF), or avtur, is a type of aviation fuel designed for use in aircraft powered by gas-turbine engines. Jet fuel is a mixture of a large number of different hydrocarbons.

5 percent: Fuel oil. Broadly speaking, fuel oil is any liquid fuel burned in a furnace or boiler for the generation of heat or used in an engine for the generation of power, except oils having a flash point of approximately 104 °F and oils burned in cotton or wool-wick burners. In this sense, diesel is a type of fuel oil.

4 percent: Liquefied petroleum gas or liquid petroleum gas (LPG or LP gas), also referred to as simply propane or butane, are flammable mixtures of hydrocarbon gases used as fuel in heating appliances, cooking equipment, and vehicles.

It is increasingly used as an aerosol propellant and a refrigerant, replacing chlorofluorocarbons in an effort to reduce damage to the ozone layer. When specifically used as a vehicle fuel, it is often referred to as autogas.

Varieties of LPG bought and sold include mixes that are mostly propane or butane and, most commonly, mixes including both propane and butane.

LPG is prepared by refining petroleum or "wet" natural gas, and is almost entirely derived from fossil fuel sources, being manufactured during the refining of petroleum (crude oil), or extracted from petroleum or natural gas streams as they emerge from the ground. It was first produced in 1910 by Dr. Walter Snelling, and the first commercial products appeared in 1912. It currently provides about 3 percent of all energy consumed, and burns relatively cleanly with no soot and very few sulfur emissions. As it is a gas, it does not pose ground or water pollution hazards, but it can cause air pollution.

The remaining **18 percent** consists of several products, including:

Kerosene, also known as lamp oil, is a combustible hydrocarbon liquid widely used as a fuel in industry and households. Before the creation of the automotive industry and the concurrent need for gasoline, kerosene was the primary derivative of crude oil.

Kerosene is widely used to power some rocket engines, and is also commonly used as a cooking and lighting fuel. In parts of Asia, where the price of kerosene is subsidized, it fuels outboard motors on small fishing boats. World total kerosene consumption for all purposes is equivalent to about 1.2 million barrels per day.

Lubricating oils, there are several types, but very generically speaking, these are oils that lubricate engines in autos and other vehicles and machines.

Paraffin wax is a white or colorless soft solid derivative from petroleum, coal or oil shale. It is solid at room temperature and begins to melt above approximately 99 degrees Fahrenheit. Common applications for paraffin wax include lubrication, electrical insulation, and candles. It is distinct from kerosene, another petroleum product sometimes called paraffin.

Paraffin candles are odorless, and bluish-white in color. Paraffin wax was first created in the 1850s, and marked a major advancement in candle-making technology, as it burned more cleanly and reliably than tallow candles, and cheaper to produce.

Asphalt, occasionally also known as bitumen, is a sticky, black and highly viscous liquid or semi-solid form of petroleum. The primary use (70 percent) of asphalt/bitumen is road construction, where it is used as the glue or binder mixed with aggregate particles to create asphalt concrete. Its other main uses are for bituminous waterproofing products, including production of roofing felt and for sealing flat roofs. The terms asphalt and bitumen are often used interchangeably to mean both natural and manufactured forms of the substance.

Petroleum coke, often abbreviated pet coke or petcoke, is a carbonaceous solid delivered from oil refinery coker units or other cracking processes. Coking is one of several refining processes.

Natural Gas Processing

Like crude oil, natural gas does not go to market in its natural state. Natural-gas processing is a complex industrial process designed to clean raw natural gas by separating impurities and various **non-methane hydrocarbons** and fluids to produce what is known as pipeline quality dry natural gas.

Natural-gas processing begins at the well head. The composition of the raw natural gas extracted from producing wells depends on the type, depth, and location of the underground deposit and the geology of the area. Oil and natural gas are often found together in the same reservoir. The natural gas produced from oil wells is generally classified as associated-dissolved, meaning the natural gas is associated with or dissolved in crude oil. Natural gas production absent of any association with crude oil is classified as "non-associated." In 2009, 89 percent of U.S. wellhead production of natural gas was non-associated.

Natural-gas processing plants purify raw natural gas by removing common contaminants such as water, **carbon dioxide** and hydrogen sulfide. Some of the substances which contaminate natural gas have economic value and are further processed or sold. A fully operational plant delivers pipeline-quality dry natural gas that can be used as fuel by residential, commercial and industrial consumers.

Quality Means Value

Oil found in reserves around the globe is not equal. Unique characteristics matter when it comes to value, pricing and refining. The more refining required to make it useful, the less value it has from the onset.

Crude oil is comprised mostly of hydrocarbon molecules and comes in many variations, colors, weights and consistencies. Density classifications (how heavy or light the oil is) were set by the American Petroleum Institute, or API, in the 1920s to provide an industry-wide standard for determining oil quality. These oil classifications, which range from light to extra heavy depending on the "weight" or API gravity, ensure consistency and fairness across the industry, and help determine market value. The higher the concentration of hydrocarbons contained in oil, the lighter it is and the less processing it needs. And, generally speaking, lighter oil is more valuable than heavier, denser oil.

API gravity of crude is calculated by figuring the ratio of its density in relation to the specific gravity of water at 60 degrees F.

$$\text{API gravity} = (141.5/\text{Specific Gravity}) - 131.5$$

API gravity classification ranges are: light (greater than 31.1), medium (from 22.3 to 31.1), heavy (below 22.3) or extra heavy (below 10).

Also, the approximate number of barrels of oil per metric ton can be determined by its API gravity.

API gravity is one of the determining factors for crude oil benchmarks for buying and selling. Crude oil benchmarks serve as reference points for determining oil price contracts. In addition to the quality of the oil, some other factors in play for determining price are the production stability of a particular field/region, transportation costs and accessibility, adequate storage facilities, and a transparent, free-flowing market.

Hundreds of benchmarks exist in the global oil market, but the three chief benchmarks are: West Texas Intermediate, Brent Crude, and Dubai Crude.

West Texas Intermediate is light, "sweet" (low sulfur) crude, having an API gravity of about 39 to 40. As its name suggests, it was first and most widely drilled in the Permian Basin in Texas, and also comes from locations throughout the southern United States, and sent via pipeline to the refinery in Cushing, Oklahoma. Crude prices in the United States are negotiated based off West Texas Intermediate oil. Its contracts are traded on the New York Mercantile Exchange.

Brent Crude is drilled offshore from four different fields in the North Sea. It also is considered light, "sweet" crude, but it is slightly heavier than West Texas Intermediate, having an API gravity of about 38. The majority of market prices are set based on Brent Crude. Oil futures for Brent Crude are bought and sold on ICE Futures Europe.

Dubai Crude is light and "sour." It has an API gravity of 31 and is high in sulfur concentrations. Dubai Crude is used for determining oil prices from the Persian Gulf and several Middle East regions, especially with delivery to areas across Asia. It is traded on the Dubai Mercantile Exchange.

Crude contracts specify the quality of the oil as well as the location from where it is derived.

Unlike oil, which has its prices determined by the global market, natural gas prices are set regionally.

Even the smallest of factors can affect prices. The amount of natural gas production is the major factor in play—the more gas produced at a given time, the lower the price. Increases or decreases due to many factors, including the weather, petroleum prices, and the overall state of the economy also have an impact.

We Don't Refine Oil or Gas

Most companies like Wright Drilling do not do any actual refining of the hydrocarbons we pull from the earth. We're like the vast majority of other gas and oil exploration companies in that regard. We sell our oil and gas to refining companies, who in turn sell the refined oil or processed gas products to their customers.

Basically, once the product is on the way to the refinery or processing plant, our involvement with it is done, other than receiving payment from the refinery.

Now that you know the entire process from beginning to end, you may wonder how you can get involved in this flourishing business. We cover that in the next chapter.

Advantages of Investing in Oil and Gas

Tax Benefits for Oil and Gas Investors

The U.S. government is actively attempting to reduce our country's dependence on foreign oil. Increased domestic drilling to enhance our own oil reserves is necessary to make this happen, and the administration is taking steps to stimulate that action. The federal government's approach to making this happen is not with huge oil giants; instead, it rests largely on the yields of many small-scale, private-source oil and gas producers. Natural gas, formed and found with oil reserves, has been successful in this area. More than half of all drilling rigs in the United States produce both oil and natural gas and, since 2009, the U.S. has been the leading natural gas producer in the world.

The IRS, identifying the importance and intricacies of tax situations in this field, developed the Oil and Gas Industry Handbook to detail the multitude of tax benefits available to investors in the oil and gas market. A section from the tax handbook overview, presented below, expresses the significance of the oil and gas industry to the country's economy:

"The oil and gas industry is one of the largest and most important segments of the U.S. economy. Due to the size and complexity of the industry, some basic examination guidelines are needed to assist examiners...

The importance of the petroleum industry to the economy of the United States has led Congress to pass specialized tax laws that are unique to the oil and gas industry. Petroleum industry accounting records have been adapted to the specialized nature of the industry."

Congress has offered oil and gas investors and small producers (companies producing below 50,000 barrels a day) some of the most attractive tax incentives available in the U.S. tax code today, something unmatched in any other industry. With these substantial tax breaks, oil and gas investing has never looked better.

Depletion allowances are some of the best tax advantages available to small producers and their investors, made possible with the Enhanced Oil Recovery Credit.

Two deduction allowances are available: cost depletion or percentage depletion. These deductions are available only to those with domestic oil and gas holdings.

Cost depletion deductions can be taken annually over the life of the well. They are derived from the actual return made from the sales of its production. Cost depletion costs apply to capitalized expenses such as the lease purchase price and legal and other professional fees associated with a producing property.

Here's an example of how this works: Landowner A recently inherited 400 acres of property from his father. Upon his father's death, the value of the land stepped up to its fair market value of

$2,500 per acre. The total value of the land is $1 million. The landowner heard of the Marcellus Shale boom from his cousins in Pennsylvania, so he allocates a portion of the land's basis to the mineral rights. He establishes a basis in the mineral rights of his royalty interest to be $80,000. Through a geological survey, it was determined there is 4,000 million cubic feet (Mmcf) of natural gas reserves. In the first year, the well produced 400 Mmcf.

The first step to calculate the cost depletion is to calculate the value for each depletion unit. This is calculated by dividing the adjusted basis of the reserves by the total reserve units. In this example, the landowner would divide $80,000 by 4,000 Mmcf, which equals $20 per Mmcf or $0.02/Mcf. In the first year, 400 Mmcf of gas were sold. For this amount, the cost depletion value is (400 Mmcf times $20/Mmcf) is $8,000. Since this is less than his cost basis of $80,000, he can deduct $8,000 for his cost depletion on Schedule E. His adjusted basis for the next tax year will be $72,000, eligible for cost depletion.

Percentage depletion allows for deductions of a percentage of income from a property. Actual costs are not considered when figuring this deduction, meaning deductions can exceed the total cost involved with acquiring the project, but cannot exceed the total amount of taxable income earned from its yields. Only small producers and investors are allowed to claim the deduction for as long as their oil or gas well generates income and it is dependent on each investor's personal financial affairs.

Here are two examples of how this works:

Example 1 — A farmer receives royalty income of $12,055, which is the only income received from his real estate. He has a taxable income from all other sources of $30,000. To calculate his percentage depletion, the farmer first multiplies the royalty income of $12,055 by the specified percentage of 15 percent, which equals $1,808. He then determines if his deduction will be limited by the 65 percent taxable rule. In this example, he takes his taxable income of $30,000 multiplied by 65 percent, which equals $19,500. Because $1,808 is smaller than $19,500, his deletion would not be limited. His depletion deduction would be $1,808 and placed on line 18 of Schedule E.

Example 2 — Betty receives royalty income of $50,000, which is the only income received from her real estate. She has a taxable income from all sources of $125,000. To calculate her percentage depletion, Betty first multiplies the royalty income of $50,000 by the specified percentage of 15 percent, which equals $7,500. She then sees if this amount is limited by the 65 percent income rule. To do this, she multiplies her taxable income of $125,000 by 65 percent, which equals $81,250. Since $7,500 is smaller than her $81,250 limit, she can deduct the entire $7,500 on line 18 on Schedule E.

Tangible and Intangible Costs

Another tax benefit of great value to oil and gas investors are those associated with tangible and intangible costs. For tax purposes, the expenses associated with drilling and developing an oil and gas well are split between either tangible or intangible costs.

Tangible drilling costs relate to the actual direct cost of the drilling equipment. These expenses are also 100 percent deductible, but must be depreciated over seven years.

Intangible drilling costs include everything but the actual drilling equipment. This would consist of labor, chemicals, mud, grease and other miscellaneous items necessary for drilling. These expenses typically represent between 65 and 80 percent of the total cost of drilling a well. They are 100 percent deductible in the year incurred.

Many of the administrative and operational costs including administrative, accounting, sales, legal, lease costs and lease operating are all 100-percent tax-deductible, as well.

Another special income tax exemption available to oil and gas well partners is the option to not only deduct the entire portion of their total investment dollars, but to also use that deduction to offset any additional income, no matter the source. This is unique to the oil and gas tax laws. Where other career fields and industries are allowed to take passive income losses as deductions, these amounts will only apply to income arising from the source. For example, investment in rental property can only apply to the revenue generated from that business. But oil and gas expenses paid out by an investor can be deducted from any income made from the investment, plus any and all other types of income, <u>including</u> wages.

These are just a few of the examples of the tremendous tax benefits available to oil and natural gas stakeholders and proof that this industry is protected by one of the rare remaining tax shelters allowable in the United States. This type of income protection means an investment in oil and natural gas today is not only a smart strategy for any investor looking for security for the immediate future, it also provides a safety net for long-term financial stability.

Another of the major benefits of investing in oil and gas projects is the residual income opportunity.

Residual Income

Residual income is one of the main advantages about oil and gas investing. While active income is earned as the fruits of our labor, where work is performed then payment received for that specific task or time. Residual income, however, is the result of performing an act (work or investment) <u>once</u> and having that act pay back in the form of <u>numerous</u> or ongoing returns long after completion.

Residual income is something everyone should strive to attain. In fact, I think high schools should teach students about importance of residual income and how to make it work for them. The residual income opportunities available from oil and gas were absolutely a motivating factor behind why I became involved in this industry initially. And those opportunities can amount to unbelievable returns.

Beyond the tax benefits available, a partner in an oil and gas venture has multiple opportunities to receive a return on the capital put forth to fund a particular project. Residual income is provided by the monthly or quarterly (or whatever time frame is outlined in the partnership contract) distributions from the sale of the product. The length of time a well remains viable, and the amounts of production that can be expected vary from project to project. But when involved in a well-managed and properly structured project, an investor should be able to expect to receive the money they put up, plus an equitable return on top.

Revenue received from processed oil is distributed to the oil and gas exploration companies from the refineries directly to the limited liability company set up for each project. The oil and gas companies, in turn, send the refinery revenues to the partners based on their ownership interests.

Oil and gas companies' accounting months are 30.4 days. Revenues are typically paid to partners a month in arrears.

Deals for investors come in all shapes and sizes. We cover some of the ways of participating in the oil and gas industry as an investor in the next chapter.

Participating Directly in Oil & Gas

In my opinion, there's no other business to be in than oil and gas. It's absolutely solid. In the case of a wildly successful product such as the iPhone, what sells this year will not sell 10 years from now. Nobody wants the 10-year-old version, so Apple has to continue to innovate and improve the product. Oil and gas isn't like that. It's good today, and it will be good 10 years from now. It's an absolute, guaranteed need for consumers. It's as essential as food and water, so there's always going to be a market for it.

An investment in this industry today is not only a smart strategy for an investor who has immediate financial goals in mind; it is also, without question, the best industry in which to be involved for long-term fiscal stability as well. A diversified oil and gas portfolio, when invested in the right team, can create growth over time unrivaled by any other industry. Investors have a range of options to consider with oil and natural gas, depending on their preferred level of involvement, risk level, and desired tax incentives.

There's a misconception out there that the oil and gas business is only for the super-wealthy. You can actually invest in oil and gas through your Individual Retirement Account. There are a lot of different ways to obtain a stake in oil and gas.

But my recommended way is through direct participation.

Direct Participation

Direct participation is an attractive investment vehicle for partners looking for solid returns on investment and valuable tax benefits. I recommend limited liability companies. Each one of our projects is a separate limited liability company. From a tax standpoint, it is structured to provide investors with the best benefits.

This type of business entity is normally formed to privately fund oil and gas well exploration, development, and operations. A company, like mine, will organize and lead the project as well as oversee the day-to-day operations. Investors provide capital upfront to fund the venture and receive revenue in the form of distributions throughout the term of the project.

You must be an accredited investor to get involved in oil and gas limited partnerships. An accredited investor is one with a special status under financial regulation laws. Generally, accredited investors include high-net-worth individuals, banks, and other large corporations who have access to complex and higher-risk investments such as venture capital, hedge funds and angel investments.

The purpose of the accredited investor status designation is to protect potential investors from risk. The assumption underlying the accreditation is that individuals or organizations who qualify will have sufficient financial sophistication to understand and take on the risks associated with certain investment offerings.

The Securities and Exchange Commission sets the criteria and restrictions on who qualifies as an accredited investor. Currently, an annual income of $200,000 or more for individuals and $300,000 for joint investors is required. Or, an individual or joint (with spouse) net worth in excess of $1 million, excluding home values, qualifies as an accredited investor. These investments are typically larger and can be riskier than those that offer smaller returns. However, these investments typically offer larger payouts.

This is a protection against someone not financially sophisticated going out and getting people's Social Security checks and investing that money. You have to be accredited to fully comprehend the risks. When you do, you can go out and get involved in investment, which ends up being a partnership because that's the way my business is organized.

With all of this in mind, you may be ready to get started. We have the roadmap for you next.

How to Get Started

The fact that you have reached this point in the book tells me you have a high degree of interest in investing in the oil and gas business. The way to get started is relatively straightforward, and here is the process I recommend:

Educate Yourself

Reading this book and learning about the industry is a great start. As I mentioned earlier, reading is something that often immerse myself in. There is no such thing as learning too much about a subject you are interested in—and in particular, one in which you are considering investing some of your own money.

If this book is your first peek at the particulars of this business, that is great. I'm glad to have had a role in helping you gain some insight. This book is designed as a primer to what you need to know to make intelligent decisions about what level of involvement you would like to entertain. I encourage you to find as much additional material as you can about oil and gas exploration, and avail yourself of it.

Part of educating yourself is being aware of the risk-and-reward elements of this business.

Risk and Reward

We've talked a lot about the risks involved in the oil and gas exploration industry in this book. To me, the biggest risk in any business is when you write a check, hand that over to somebody, and let that person be responsible for your financial well-being. That's a *major* risk. There are a lot of professionals, in a lot of professions, who can help you make proper decisions that are best for your business. When it comes down to it, Mother Nature is always in charge. You hire all these pros, they go out and make the proper decisions, they decide this is where you need to drill, and this is how far you need to drill, and you let all that happen. But we can't control the weather, and we can't control what's in that ground. You go out and get those pros to do the best possible job possible under the circumstances.

Your biggest risk in the oil and gas business is partnering with the proper company. There are a lot of folks out there who can talk the business, but in the end, don't do it. There are a lot of companies that tell you what they're going to do, but really have no intentions of doing that. You have to know, as an investor/partner, who you're getting in business with. That's another reason for this book. Not only does it educate you about in oil and gas, it tells you who's involved in this business.

While the risks are by now abundantly clear to you, the potential rewards are what make it an amazing business. I have been involved in oil and gas accounting since 1994, and I've done a lot of oil and gas tax returns for many landowners who have mineral rights and royalties—lots of different types of oil money coming in. There is one particular family I remember for whom I had been doing tax returns for a good 16 to 17 years.

When the mother passed away, her oil royalties went to two daughters. Now one of those daughters has passed away, and that daughter has two daughters. We're on the third generation of oil and gas money from a husband and wife making an investment in the business 40 to 50 years ago. That family continues to reap the rewards, and reaping in a big-time way. We're not talking about a $300 or $400 check coming in each month. We're now on third-generation heirs to an oil and gas investment in west Texas back in the 1960s and 70s.

Any time there is high risk, there is also a high reward. You put a decent amount of money into a well, and in this day and age, when leases and drilling are a little cheaper, a person could invest $100,000, and replace his or her income overnight. That is the kind of reward that can result from the oil and gas business. You do that over several times, and those are the kinds of things that are life-changing, legacy-changing. You've built yourself quite an estate. Your heirs can live off those proceeds. There is risk, but there is great reward, too.

Managing Risk

How do you determine the right amount? Well, if you're doing something that's really risky in exploration, it's hard to quantify.

You have to figure out what's the real risk on the exploration. All of it has risk. There isn't anything that's an absolute guaranteed thing. Even when it looks like a sure thing, there are all kinds of mechanical problems that can occur, even on a simple, vertical well.

Firms like ours get project partners not only for their capital, but also because of their need to manage risk. Other potential partners understand that, and they are open to joint ventures because everyone understands mitigating the risk is an important part of this business.

An example of how this mindset works: You've got a well that will cost $1 million to drill. While you have $1 million available, you're only comfortable putting $100,000 at risk. So, you invest with other partners in the oil and gas venture, leaving you additional capital to invest in other projects. The goal: diversification.

Very few companies in this business want 100 percent of the risk. They don't want to be too exposed on any one project.

Due Diligence

Before embarking on any financial investment, whether oil or otherwise, your top priority should be to conduct your own due diligence and fully vet any projects. It can be very easy for a company to "sell" a project through fancy marketing or by making it appear to be a sure thing. But in oil and gas, there are no sure things and the level of risk associated with any project should always be investigated. Any dealings with an operator/project manager who downplays any chance of risks in a project should be approached with caution.

One of the most important things to look for when investing in an oil and gas venture is transparency. Companies that offer maximum disclosure and openly provide the information needed about its team members, investment materials, business practices, financial standings, deal structures, and any other documentation, will allow potential investors to properly assess their risks before making deals. Open lines of communication are vital. If you are investing thousands and thousands of dollars of your money into a project, you should get the clearest picture possible of who and what you'll be involved. Your answers should be answered quickly and honestly. Any deviation on this should send up a red flag and make you reconsider your options.

Legitimate oil and gas companies should have no issue with providing the clearest view of all parts of the business and project. But it is important to remember it is your responsibility to verify even those that are forthcoming and open with their operations. It is your money and remaining diligent concerning investments allows you to make the best decisions with your finances.

We believe in bringing our partners in to let them be a part of the process. We open ourselves up in ways that many companies would never do. We recently launched a website that serves as a portal for investors seeking to gain additional information on the company or get real-time updates on current projects. We have even installed cameras at all of our work sites that stream live online 24 hours a day and can be viewed easily by logging in on the website.

The oil and gas industry is inherently technical and often many risks are completely out of the hands of the company seeking the support of partners. But an area where an investor has control over the risks involved in oil and gas deals is in choosing a trustworthy company with which they do business. Appropriate past management strategies and risk planning is where reputable companies stand out. Fervent oil companies stay ahead of the game by monitoring project-specific threats and working to minimize those risks.

No matter the uncertainty of future prices or how unstable the current state of the market, an oil and gas producer has the ability to remain poised for success through solid business principles. A wise producer will attain this by ensuring financial stability from the onset by preparing for price and/or demand fluctuations, and securing a niche by locking-in demand with long-term, strategic relationships.

How We Operate

Wright Drilling focuses on creating limited liability companies, as I believe it offers the best tax incentives and potential residual income opportunities.

Each one of our wells is an independent joint venture limited liability company in itself. Well "A" might have five partners. Well "B" might have two people who get involved. Each one of the wells is an independent, joint-venture, LLC, which I think is a phenomenal way to do business.

And why should you, as a potential partner, join Wright Drilling instead of one of the numerous other very reputable oil and gas exploration companies? I'm a businessman. I'm an accountant by trade. I've had wonderful success—26 years in the accounting business—but I am a businessman. What successful businesspeople do is surround themselves with highly-educated intelligent people who can make proper decisions for them.

I'm not a petroleum engineer. Therefore, I find the best petroleum engineers possible. I'm not a geologist. I'm not a land man. I'm not an oil and gas operator. I find the guys who can do those things, and when I find them, I let them do their job. Sometimes, that even means that geologist telling me, "You need to plug this hole because there's no oil there. You need to move on to the next one. You need to cut your costs and move on."

You can't continue chasing ideas that make no business sense. When Wright Drilling sets up a program or a project, we've already done all the intelligent decision-making to minimize your risk—because as we have emphasized time and again throughout this book, there is risk in the oil and gas business.

Become Our Partner

You probably understand that one of the primary goals of this book, along with informing you about this industry, is to pique your interest in Wright Drilling. If, after you have read this book, you feel like my company might be a good fit for you, I would love the opportunity to get to know you and learn more about your objectives. You can contact me by visiting my website at http://wrightdrilling.com. Look for the "contact us" link in the navigation bar at the top of the page. Just fill out the form, submit it, and we will be back in contact with you shortly.

Looking Ahead

We've talked a lot in this book about the technological advances that have reinvigorated the oil and gas exploration industry, particularly in the United States. We may not have seen anything yet.

The reasons why I believe this industry is the best option for a wise investor are clear. And not only that, they continue to expand as technology does the same. I hope that as you finish this book, the reasons for you to be an interested investor are clear.

Likewise, I hope to have impressed upon you the steps I have taken to make Wright Drilling particularly worthy of your consideration. I invite you to use what you have learned and reach out to me and my professional team. We would be very interested in discussing you becoming a partner in our growing endeavor in an industry that has no end in sight.

Go out and take advantage of the opportunity for which you are now ready. If you don't, you'll see this book on a shelf in 10 years and wonder, "What if?"

Don't let that happen. Now is your time.

How to Contact Us

Wright Drilling & Exploration, Inc.
Oil & Gas Investment Opportunities
120 S. Austin Ave, #101
Denison, TX 75020

T: 214-447-0202

E: info@wrightdrilling.com

Want More Information?

Wright Drilling & Exploration, Inc. holds frequent webinars on oil & gas investing topics and to answer questions. Visit www.oilgasinvestments.com for more information.

Made in the USA
Monee, IL
09 June 2023